00

For Aunt Vernette,
with much love,
John Conde
10-31-85

Cars With Personalities

BY JOHN A. CONDE

The Cars That Hudson Built (1980)

Cars With Personalities

by John A. Conde

Arnold-Porter
Publishing Company

Keego Harbor, Michigan 48033

To
my son Jeff
and
my daughter Cam

Contents

About the Photographs

Most of the photographs are credited, as they
appear, to the sources from which the author
obtained them. MVMA is an abbreviation for
Motor Vehicle Manufacturers Association. If no
credit line is given, the picture is from the
author's collection.

Preface

I have always been fascinated by pictures of celebrities with automobiles which I began collecting solely for the fun of it about twenty years ago. Photographs of this kind are appealing not only because of the famous persons shown but also because special cars usually are involved, sometimes models with exotic custom bodies. In a broader sense, these pictures reflect the times in which the cars and personalities were contemporary. The backgrounds often are as interesting as the cars and the notables themselves. Some show recognizable streets, buildings, homes or commercial establishments. All show fashions and hair styles of the times.

The search for pictures of this type took many years and the photographs came from a variety of sources. During my long tenure at American Motors I found perhaps fifty photos of prominent individuals with Nash, Hudson, Essex, Terraplane and Willys-Overland cars. From the Motor Vehicle Manufacturers Association I borrowed pictures showing celebrities with other car makes. From Stanley Yost, then living in Royal Oak, Michigan, I obtained a dozen or so photos of notables with cars built early in the century. Others came through my contacts with General Motors, Ford and Chrysler.

A substantial boost to my collection came in 1971 when a longtime friend, Al G. Waddell, then past eighty, gave me hundreds of original photographs that he had saved over a long career in the newspaper and public relations fields, extending as far back as 1914 when he became auto editor of *The Los Angeles Times*. Included were a number of superb pictures of Hollywood film stars with automobiles.

Al's wonderful contribution whetted my interest to obtain more pictures, so I began to ask for them at antique car meets and to write to fellow photo enthusiasts. Additional excellent pictures of Hollywood stars with automobiles came from Tony Mitchell in California. For many years I had been sending pictures of American Motors cars to George A. Moffitt, of New York, who has collected automobile photos for several decades. When he learned of my interest, he provided numerous additional pictures.

The real impetus, however, that spurred my growing conviction that an interesting and unique book could be developed using the photographs I had gathered came less than a year ago. I joined with three other graduates of the automobile industry in volunteering to help sort the thousands of negatives and photographs that were donated by the Packard Motor Car Company to the Detroit Public Library. Because of a lack of staff and space, this huge collection had remained in piles of boxes since their arrival at the library back in 1955. When several of us who are members of the Board of Trustees of the library's National Automotive History Collection volunteered to examine and sort the photographs and negatives (almost all of which are identified only with negative numbers, with no usable index), I found more than 140 superb photographs of Packard cars with celebrities. Many are included in this book, thanks to the alertness of my volunteer associates — John R. McAlpine, veteran of fifty years in the automobile advertising business who was with Packard's advertising agency, Young & Rubicam, from 1940 to 1947; Joseph H. Karshner, who spent thirty-one years with General Motors public relations, handling important assignments for the news relations section, and Stanley H. Brams, longtime Detroit editor of several national business magazines and publisher of *Detroit Labor Trends*.

A few comments about the pictures used in the book are in order. The cars are presented in chronological order even if the pictures might have been taken later. For example, a photo of President Coolidge in a 1921 Pierce-

Arrow was taken in 1923, after he took office. Certain personalities appear a number of times in a number of different cars. In this category are Thomas A. Edison, Buffalo Bill, Jack Dempsey, Al Jolson, Dolores Del Rio, Clark Gable, "Cannon Ball" Baker and Barney Oldfield.

Acknowledgments

I am very grateful to a host of individuals and organizations for the help I received in the preparation of this book. I am especially indebted to Hendrik C. Kranendonk, of Muiderberg, Holland, for the many hours he devoted to pinpointing the model designations and years of most of the Packard photographs; to James K. Wagner for lending his expertise in correctly identifying cars built by Ford Motor Company; to Thomas C. Van Degrift, Jr., for making prints from fragile old negatives, and for his counsel. To James Wren and Bernice Huffman, of the Motor Vehicle Manufacturers Association, my deepest thanks for helping me locate elusive pictures and for providing background information from the Association's vast files.

Special thanks go also to Val Almendarez, of the Academy of Motion Picture Arts and Sciences; John Redding, of the National Baseball Hall of Fame; Skip Marketti and Gregg Buttermore, of the Auburn-Cord-Duesenberg Museum; Jack Martin and Ron McQueeney, of the Indianapolis Motor Speedway; Ted Koehler, Gene Jendrasik and Thomas P. Saunders, of GM Photographic; Lou Halverson and Dolores Axam, of the Free Library of Philadelphia; Max-Gerritt Von Pein, director of the Daimler-Benz Museum in Stuttgart; Marcus Clary, of Mercedes-Benz of North America; William J. Vollmar, archives manager, Anheuser-Busch Companies; Douglas Bakken, David Crippen, Cynthia Read, Donald W. Matteson, Randy Mason, Wanda Karavas, Ross Kalloway and David Wojack, of the Henry Ford Museum; Richard Scharchburg, of General Motors Institute; Dale Gilchrist, Tom Ciemiega, Richard A. Teague and Loretta Mullins, of American Motors Corporation; Otto Rosenbusch and Carla Rosenbusch, of Chrysler Historical Collection; Norb Bartos, of Cadillac Motor Car Division; Helen Earley, of Oldsmobile Division; Richard Quinn, Howard and Shelby Applegate, Fred K. Fox and Herb Read, Studebaker historians; Thomas H. Hubbard and Walter E. Gosden, Franklin historians; Jack Miller, former president of the Hudson-Essex-Terraplane Club; Perry E. Piper and David Babb, of the Edsel Owners Club; John Philip Atkins, Beverly Ferreira, Richard Day, John M. Lauter, Dudley Morrison and Linda Seebach, of the Packard Club; John C. Curry, of the Michigan State Archives; Sandy Sandula, Gloria Francis, Margaret Butzu, Paul Scupholm and the late James J. Bradley, of the National Automotive History Collection, Detroit Public Library; Jeff Gillis, of the Durant Family Registry; W. Denney Freeston, of the Willys-Overland-Knight Registry, and Henry Austin Clark, Jr., a wonderful friend who provided a number of priceless early photographs.

Finally, for their assistance and counsel, I wish to thank William L. Bailey, Calvin Beauregard, Richard I. Braund, Carl W. Burst III, Craig Farley, Charlie Gehringer, Graydon Hauser, Robert Hunter, Beverly Rae Kimes, Thomas F. Lerch, David L. Lewis, Robert Mehl, Hans J. Mueller, Mrs. Henry Dutton Noble, George Risley, Kathy Sgro, William F. Sherman, Lorin Sorensen, G. Whitney Snyder, Richard H. Stout, C. M. Terry, James W. Watson and Ted Weems, Jr.

JOHN A. CONDE
BLOOMFIELD HILLS, MICHIGAN
OCTOBER 1, 1982

1896-1905: *Getting Started*

O n October 17, 1895, the governor of Ohio who was to become president of the United States, William McKinley, told the Carriage Builders national convention in Cleveland: "The trend of the times is to get on wheels." He was addressing manufacturers of horse-drawn vehicles, but many of them already were expressing alarm at the growing interest Americans were displaying in horseless carriages.

Even those far-sighted builders of horse-drawn vehicles who eventually converted to automobile production, however, believed the market for the new-fangled machines would always be restricted to wealthier owners. In fact, in the decade beginning in 1896, not much happened to dispute the contention. If anything, evidence continued to mount that the automobile, being complicated and requiring constant attention, could not be maintained and operated by an ordinary motorist, even if he were rich. So most owners had chauffeurs, who often also were excellent mechanics.

Many of the automobiles sold in this period, despite high import tariffs, were expensive, large, high-powered models built in Europe. American manufacturers, on the other hand, were experimenting in almost every area. They built cars powered by steam, by electricity and by gasoline. The engines had one cylinder, or two or three or four, and they were mounted in the front, in the middle or in the rear. Some were steered with a tiller, others by a wheel. No norms had been set because even the buyers had not decided positively what they wanted.

In this decade, the developments were many and varied. Each contributed in its own way to the personality of the motorcar in America as we know it today. The first company to build gasoline-powered automobiles, Duryea Motor Wagon Company of Springfield, Massachusetts, was in 1896 already a year old, and others quickly followed. In 1897 Gilbert Loomis, a mechanic from Westfield, Massachusetts who had built his own one-cylinder car, took out an insurance policy covering his creation. A year later the first

A typical rural small town in America, Clyde, Ohio, as it looked on a wintry Saturday afternoon in 1900 before the advent of the automobile.

"Rigs That Run" was the slogan of one of America's oldest major manufacturers of motor vehicles, the St. Louis Motor Carriage Company, whose factory in St. Louis is pictured as it looked in 1900. Its runabouts and commercial vehicles are lined up in front.

independent auto dealership was opened in Detroit by William E. Metzger. The first dealer to be franchised was H. O. Koller of Reading, Pennsylvania, who sold Winton cars. In 1899 the U.S. Post Office Department began experiments in collecting mail with motor vehicles in Buffalo, Cleveland and Washington. In Chicago, Mrs. John Howell Phillips became the first woman in the United States to receive a driver's license.

In November 1900 the first national automobile show was held in New York's Madison Square Garden. It rivaled the annual horse show as a social event, and there seemed to be as much interest in electric and steam cars as in gasoline-powered models. William McKinley followed the trend of the times as he became the first president to ride in an automobile. *The Saturday Evening Post* carried its first automobile advertising, and a steam car was driven up Pike's Peak by John Brisben Walker.

Many endurance and hill-climbing events brought curious crowds and automobile daredevils anxious to prove the reliability of their new models. A few states passed legislation, as early as 1901, regulating the speed of motor vehicles, and a new-fangled invention called a speedometer was made available as one of the first extra-cost accessories. In 1902, the same year the American Automobile Association was formed, T. H. Shevlin was arrested in Minneapolis and fined ten dollars for daring to drive ten miles per hour.

The first transcontinental automobile trips were made in the summer of 1903. Dr. H. Nelson Jackson of Burlington, Vermont and his chauffeur Sewall K. Crocker drove a Winton from San Francisco to New York, departing May 23 and arriving in Manhattan July 26. Leaving San Francisco June 20, Tom Fetch drove a one-cylinder Packard (known as "Old Pacific") across the country in fifty-three days. Finally, L.

L. Whitman and C. T. Hammond in an Oldsmobile made the same trip, leaving July 6 and arriving September 17.

The automobile was beginning to look less each year like a carriage without a horse. Americans were beginning to accept the permanent reality of motorcars even if they were noisy and smelly (unless they were slow-moving but elegant electrics), and even if they could not be driven with assurance in the winter-time, and even if there were no paved roads outside the larger cities, and even if they were too expensive for the average family.

With what limited leisure time they had, however, most Americans found ways to have a good time without the luxury of owning automobiles. In the predominant rural areas, they went to town on Saturdays in the wagon or buggy. They listened to band concerts in the town square, and sometimes they saw a traveling carnival or circus. In the summer there were the county fair, church bazaars and ice-cream socials. In the cities, they listened to the gramaphone and witnessed the miracle of moving pictures in nickelodeons. They rode the trolleys into the heart of the city to shop, to attend church, concerts or a baseball game. Back home, sitting on the front porch swing, they might even see in their newspapers or in one of the new automobile trade journals pictures of automobiles with famous people . . . cars with personalities.

Early motoring had its hazards. Many small streams and rivers in America, while they might have foot bridges across them, had no bridges for vehicles. Horse-drawn wagons and carriages generally found a shallow place and forded the stream, as this Franklin car is doing.

The first automobile to appear on the streets of Detroit was this gasoline-powered vehicle designed and built by Charles Brady King (right). With mechanic Oliver E. Barthel as his passenger, King propelled the crude-looking car on Woodward Avenue on March 6, 1896. King had road-tested the four-cylinder vehicle at night prior to its historic public bow. He went on to design the Detroit-built Northern automobile and founded the King Motor Car Company which lasted from 1911 to 1924.

MVMA

COMMENTARY

One of the most interesting assignments I had during my thirty-two years with American Motors and its predecessor, Nash-Kelvinator Corporation, happened less than a year after I began working for the Detroit-based company.

In the spring of 1946, I was selected to be the official aide to one of the living pioneers of the auto industry who were to be honored during the Automotive Golden Jubilee in Detroit. He was Charles Brady King, then seventy-eight and living in retirement in Larchmont, New York.

The Jubilee was a happy event promoted by the Automobile Manufacturers Association to stimulate Detroit's labor-management climate which was sagging because of repeated wildcat strikes and the removal of wartime wage and price controls. The idea of inviting the most prominent automotive pioneers to participate was a mild stroke of genius. Some of the greatest men the motor industry ever produced were still alive, and all were invited: Henry Ford, Ransom E. Olds, Charles W. Nash, William C. Durant, Alfred P. Sloan, J. Frank Duryea, Edgar L. Apperson, George Holley, Barney Oldfield — and Charles Brady King, the man who drove the first car seen on the streets of Detroit in 1896. (Others honored were John Zaugg, veteran White Motor Company worker; Frank Kwilinski, veteran Studebaker worker; Charles S. Snyder, oldtime White and Hudson dealer, and John Van Benschoten, pioneer Dodge dealer.)

Each automobile company was asked to provide

someone to serve as an aide to a pioneer — to accompany him to all functions, keep him on schedule and provide any and all services to make his appearance in Detroit grand and memorable. Henry Ford's aide was his young grandson, Henry Ford II. Godfrey Strelinger, treasurer of Nash-Kelvinator, was aide to Charles W. Nash. And I was aide to Charles B. King.

Because the Jubilee schedule was crowded and hectic, the aides were given periodic briefings by Perry TeWalt, of the AMA staff, who cautioned that the pioneers were "old and feeble," and that it was our job to monitor their every move. It was with a mixture of fear and suspense, therefore, that I looked forward to my first meeting with Mr. King.

We were provided with the use of a 1946 Nash Ambassador sedan and a company driver, whose sole task during the week of the Jubilee was to drive Mr. King wherever he wanted to go, whenever that might be. He stayed with a sister in Grosse Pointe, which meant long round trips to pick him up and return him home every day.

I'll never forget my reactions when first we saw Mr. King. Tall, robust and handsome with hardly a wrinkle on his face, he greeted us at the door of his sister's home: "Come in, gentlemen," he said briskly, "and have a cup of coffee while I finish some correspondence I started around six this morning."

Old and feeble indeed! Charles Brady King was ready and eager to take on any assignment given to him by Jubilee officials. No one needed to tell him he was the center of attention in practically every activity. Because he had been the first to drive a car in Detroit half a century earlier, his appearances were more in demand than those of any other pioneer. I therefore had to keep pace with him as we made hurried trips to newspaper offices and radio stations. He was interviewed on Fred Waring's network program that originated at the Olympia Stadium, as well as "The Quiz Kids" and other

This remarkable photograph of two men past eighty reminiscing at the Automotive Golden Jubilee in Detroit was taken by Marty Pierce, who was engaged by Nash-Kelvinator to make record photos of the occasion. Charles W. Nash is talking softly while Henry Ford listens.

shows. He appeared at the old Convention Hall for an exhibition of antique cars such as Detroit had never seen before. He was the key figure on the reviewing stand on Woodward Avenue for the June 1 parade that climaxed it all.

The greatest thrill for me was the opportunity Mr. King gave me to meet the other pioneers. William C. Durant and Alfred P. Sloan were unable to attend, but he introduced me to Ransom Olds, Barney Oldfield (always with a cigar), Charles Nash and the others. I could not help observing that "the others" seemed much older than the vigorous Charles B. King.

After several days of frantic activity and excitement had passed, however, we still had not seen Henry Ford. It was well known that he seldom appeared in public anymore and some speculated that he was not well (in fact, he died less than a year later). But another Jubilee highlight was about to take place — a huge banquet at the Masonic Temple. It was a black tie affair for the head-table guests, and I remember how resplendent my pioneer Charles King looked.

Before the banquet started, it was arranged that all of the pioneers were to meet in a smaller room in the Masonic Temple for a special ceremony. They were to sign their names on special white cards. Later their signatures would be emblazoned on a plaque which was to be a permanent part of an industrial wing of the proposed Detroit Historical Museum. All of the pioneers with one important exception gathered in the room, with only a few others because of the limited space. An air of anticipation quieted the group. Any moment, we all believed, Henry Ford would walk in.

Charles Brady King and John A. Conde as they looked in 1946 during the Automotive Golden Jubilee in Detroit.

Soon it happened. The door swung open and Mr. Ford walked slowly into the room, on the arm of his grandson. Suddenly everyone stopped talking, and there was an awkward silence. In all of the planning, no one apparently had decided who would greet Mr. Ford. It took only a few seconds for Charles B. King to recognize the situation. He raced across the room, his hand out, "Hi, ya, Hank!" It was the first time anyone I talked to later who heard the greeting had ever heard Mr. Ford called Hank, but he and Mr. King had been close friends and associates for more than half a century, and that's what Mr. King called him. Mr. Ford, frail and stooped — though still a handsome and distinguished man — responded with a smile, calling my pioneer "Charlie."

And then it happened. As though to apologize for taking so long, Mr. King turned to me and said: "Hank, I want you to meet my sidekick here, John Conde." I shook Mr. Ford's hand in awe, and then stepped back into the anonymity reserved for aides to automotive pioneers.

Seated primly in the first of many millions of automobiles he was to build in his lifetime is Henry Ford. He was thirty-three years old in 1896 when he completed this two-cylinder "Quadricycle," so named because it ran on four bicycle wheels. The photograph was taken soon after he drove the vehicle for the first time on the streets of Detroit on June 4, 1896.

COMMENTARY

The original 1896 Ford Quadricycle is exhibited under a special glass case in the Henry Ford Museum in Dearborn, Michigan. It is one of a number of original cars on display that Henry Ford built prior to the formation of Ford Motor Company in 1903 and the start of production of automobiles offered for public sale.

Despite the fact that Henry Ford had a keen interest in American history and wanted to preserve much of what made the automobile industry outstanding, he did not always recognize the historic importance of the very first car he built with his own hands. I was surprised to learn this during the four years (1977 to 1981) that I was curator of transportation at the Henry Ford Museum, created by Henry Ford in 1929 through establishment of the Edison Institute which also includes Greenfield Village.

It was while I was doing some fascinating research into the background of the Quadricycle, as well as 165 other motorcars in the museum collection, in preparation for the organization's fiftieth anniversary in 1979, that an interesting story unfolded. Only a few months after completing the Quadricycle and driving it on Detroit's downtown streets, Ford sold the car for $200 to Charles Ainsley. Eight years passed before Ford had a change of heart and bought the vehicle back for sixty-five dollars.

How he built and tested the Quadricycle is also most interesting. When the time arrived for the car's first road test, to his dismay Ford found that the vehicle would not fit through the door to his brick wood-shed workshop behind his home at 58 Bagley Avenue. So he removed the door frame and a few bricks and pushed the car onto the cobblestone alley behind his home. He cranked it up and, with his friend Jim Bishop bicycling alongside, Ford and his first car toured Detroit's deserted streets.

The Quadricycle has a single seat and is steered by a tiller. Ford made the two cylinders for the engine from the exhaust pipe of a steam engine. The vehicle is quite light, weighing without fuel only 500 pounds. It has two speeds, one ten and one twenty miles an hour.

Henry Ford continued to improve the vehicle for about six months, modifying the cooling system, water tank, wheels, seat and frame. He drove it about 1,000 miles.

So many demands have been placed on this frail little original car that in 1963, Ford Motor Company commissioned George DeAngelis to build an operable replica. It is this faithful reproduction of the Quadricycle that is exhibited on the floor of the museum, starting a long line of Ford-built products over the years.

OLDSMOBILE DIVISION

Automotive pioneer Ransom E. Olds is at the tiller of this experimental 1896 Oldsmobile model. Olds carved two careers in the automobile industry. He founded Oldsmobile before the turn of the twentieth century but left the firm in 1904 to form the Reo Motor Car Company of Lansing, Michigan, a year later. Besides Olds is Frank G. Clark. Behind Clark, her face partially obscured, is Olds' wife Metta; seated next to her is Mrs. Clark.

Thomas B. Jeffery is seated in his first gasoline-powered automobile. Designed and built in 1897, it was the first of many Rambler prototypes developed over a four-year period prior to the start of production at Kenosha, Wisconsin, early in 1902. Jeffery was a pioneer bicycle manufacturer and noted inventor. Among his inventions were the clincher tire and a three-wheeled railroad velocipede.

AMERICAN MOTORS CORPORATION

FREE LIBRARY OF PHILADELPHIA

At the age of sixteen, Russell Janney, who years later would become a famous author and theatrical producer, took a spin in this steam car with his two younger sisters, Ramona and Bertha. The vehicle was built in 1898 in Keene, New Hampshire by their father, who manufactured Trinity bicycles, and was the first horseless carriage seen in the area. Janney went on to carve out a distinguished career. He served as press agent for George Arliss and Theda Bara, wrote the words (together with Brian Hooker) for **The Vagabond King** and in 1947 authored the highly successful book, **The Miracle of the Bells.**

One of the leading electric cars at the turn of the twentieth century was the Baker, made in Cleveland from 1899 to 1915. Shown seated in a 1900 model are Mr. and Mrs. Thomas A. Edison. Edison lent his name to the promotion of many electrics — not entirely because he had confidence in their future but because most of them used batteries made by his company.

Carry Nation, the American temperance agitator, chose to ride in a 1901 Thomas to the first Boston automobile show with her manager, seated behind her. The driver of the tiller-operated car built in Buffalo is C.S. Henshaw. It was in Medicine Lodge, Kansas that Carry Nation (1846-1911) became convinced of her divine appointment to destroy the saloon. A year before this photograph was taken she supplemented public prayers by personal destruction of property in saloons, including the smashing of bottles and beer kegs. Later she used the hatchet as her weapon.

James Ward Packard, one of the founders of the Packard Motor Car Company, is seated in the Model C Packard roadster he drove in the New York-to-Buffalo endurance run in 1901 which was halted at Rochester by the assassination of President William McKinley. The Packard automobile, for many years America's premier luxury car, was produced over a span of fifty-nine years, from 1899 to 1958. The company was founded in Warren, Ohio, but moved to Detroit in 1904.

The best-selling car in the United States by a wide margin in 1901 was the one-cylinder Oldsmobile, with its distinctive curved dash. Priced at only $650, it was a trustworthy performer as evidenced by this photograph of Ransom E. Olds (left), founder of the company that is now Oldsmobile Division of General Motors Corporation, piloting one of his runabouts up a steep hill in Detroit. His passenger is John D. Maxwell, who three years later formed his own company in Tarrytown, New York, to build the famous Maxwell car.

Competition among automobile makers was so brisk in the pioneering period that to prove their claims of superiority, many companies actively participated in racing, endurance and other performance events. Here William K. Vanderbilt, Jr., scion of the family that made millions in the railroad business, is photographed in his imported 1902 Mors at the Eagle Rock Hill Climb in Montclair, New Jersey. The Mors was built in France from 1895 to 1925. The American Mors was produced later, from 1906 to 1909, in St. Louis.

Trying his hand at a one-cylinder 1904 Michigan runabout is William Frederick Cody, better known as Buffalo Bill, the famed American plainsman, scout and showman. "The car of power" was the slogan of the Michigan, built in Kalamazoo from 1903 to 1907. Buffalo Bill was born near Davenport, Iowa. When he was eight, his family moved to Kansas, and on his father's death in 1857, Bill set out to earn the family living, working for supply trains and a freighting company. In 1859, he went to the Colorado gold fields. In the Civil War he was an army scout on the Western border. He had many adventures then and later as a buffalo hunter.

At one time Jackson, Michigan was a major center of automobile manufacturing. In addition to Buick, Briscoe, Cutting, Earl and Imperial, a well-known make was the Jackson, built for two decades (1903-23). Early in its career it was spelled Jaxon and was offered with both steam and gasoline-powered engines. The man wearing the derby in this rare photograph of a 1904 Jaxon is William Sparks, a founder of the highly successful auto supplier firm, Sparks-Withington (fans, radiators, horns — and later refrigerators, radios and TV sets — all under the Sparton name). Sparks was known as "Cap" because of his rank as captain of the famed Jackson Zouaves.

A large delegation of adventuresome (and mostly rich) automobile owners in 1904 helped promote the emerging auto industry by driving from New York state to St. Louis where the World's Fair was being held. A leader of the tour was Charles J. Glidden, seen here with his wife on their arrival in Albany in the 1904 Napier in which they later drove around the world. The highly-regarded Napier was built in England from 1900 to 1924.

Many people tend to relate the early success of Henry Ford exclusively to the legendary Model T, but it was not introduced until October 1908. Meanwhile, the Detroit manufacturer experimented with many different designs, each bearing a letter in the alphabet. He is shown here seated next to the chauffeur of a four-cylinder 1905 Model B Ford, produced from 1904 to 1906. In the back seat is Miss Myrle Clarkson, then the office manager of Ford Motor Company.

The Model B Ford at $2,000 was far from being a low-priced car. At the same time it was on the market, so was Model C, which carried a price of $900. But a number of competing makes — the Oldsmobile, for one — sold for less. Henry Ford was unsure at this point in his career of the direction he wanted to take. In fact, in 1907 he introduced a huge six-cylinder car called Model K which proved to be somewhat of a disaster. Once the Model T was under development, he not only became convinced that his future lay in the low-priced field, but also that four cylinders were enough. All of the more than fifteen million Model Ts built from mid-1908 to 1927 were powered by the consistently dependable four-cylinder Ford engine.

Almost from the beginning of the automobile industry, one of America's leading (and therefore wealthiest) distributors was Alvan Tufts Fuller, of Boston. When this happy photograph of Fuller with his family in a 1905 Packard was taken, he was the distributor not only for Packard but also for Cadillac and Northern. He later served two terms as governor of Massachusetts (from 1925 to 1929).

COMMENTARY

What were the most popular cars in 1905? Well, for one thing, not many were sold. The exact total is unknown, but in that year only 77,400 passenger cars were registered in the United States — and that included all automobiles in use, those built in previous years as well as foreign makes. Even so, as many as 100 companies were competing for what little market existed. Figures are available, however, to indicate the ranking of cars by the totals built in the calendar year 1905. In first place by a wide margin was Oldsmobile, with 6,500 units produced. In second place was Cadillac, with 3,492 (virtually all low-priced models); then followed Rambler with 3,807, Ford with 1,599, Franklin with 1,098, White with 1,015, Reo with 864, Maxwell with 823, Buick with 750 and Stanley with 610.

Four midgets from the Barnum & Bailey Circus are sitting in the "Baby Reo," a half-size vehicle built by Reo Motor Car Company in Lansing, Michigan in its first year, 1905, and initially shown to the public a year later. The car belonged to the Reo firm for many years until its purchase in 1973 by Richard A. Teague, vice-president of styling for American Motors Corporation. Originally it was powered by compressed air so it could be operated indoors in safety, but in 1954 it was converted to gasoline power. The Reo automobile was produced from 1905 to 1936 by Ransom E. Olds (the name stands for his initials). The company continued to build trucks until 1967 when through mergers the name was changed to Diamond-Reo.

Pictured in a 1905 Mercedes Simplex is the King of Bulgaria (third from left). This classic automobile was a product of the German company founded by Karl Benz, who is credited with having designed and built in 1885 the first workable motor car driven by an internal combustion engine.

14

1906-1915: *Coming of Age*

On January 27, 1906, a phenomenal record was set on the sands of Ormond Beach, Florida that was to signal momentous changes in the automobile and the role it was to play in American society in the succeeding decade. A Stanley Steamer was driven by Fred Marriott at an average speed of 127.66 miles per hour.

The incredible feat seemed to foretell dramatic events to come, many of which directly involved the motorcar. Three months after the Stanley record was established, private passenger cars of every make were called upon to rescue hundreds of victims of the tragic earthquake and fire in San Francisco.

The automobile in the decade 1906-1915 became a better product of even greater service to owners. Better materials, mechanical improvements and more powerful engines gave the leading cars competitive advantage. In 1906 alone, five manufacturers introduced six-cylinder engines. The automobile was coming of age.

The year 1908 marked two significant milestones in the industry's young history. It was the year General Motors was organized and the year the legendary Model T Ford was introduced — the car that in reality put America on wheels. Within the next five years Ford Motor Company moved into its new, larger Highland Park plant, was turning out 1,000 cars a day and announced its revolutionary five-dollar minimum daily wage.

In 1909 the nation's first rural mile of concrete pavement was laid on Woodward Avenue in Detroit. It highlighted one of the serious problems facing motorists enthralled with the new freedom given them to go anywhere they wanted to anytime they wanted to. But most of them hesitated to go too far from home because of the deplorable state of America's roads and high-

MVMA

This remarkable photograph shows a horse expressing its feelings about an automobile as they meet at the crest of a hill near Canonsburg, Pennsylvania. The 1906 car stays as far as it can to its side of the road.

At first glance one might think this big high-powered car has been stopped by the horrible condition of the New Jersey highway after an early spring rain. However, the two women are telling the chauffeur how to persuade the dog at the right to return to the car. The time is about 1909.

ways. Many were not even marked, and while it was common practice to ask for directions from the nearest farmer, he generally could only tell the perplexed motorist how to get as far as *he* had been. Not much progress was made in this decade in attacking the roads problem.

Somehow, due largely to excellent planning, Mrs. John J. Ramsey managed in 1909 to become the first woman to cross the United States in an automobile. She left New York in a Maxwell with three women companions and arrived in San Francisco fifty-three days later.

By the end of 1909 automobiles were being produced in 145 cities in twenty-four states. A total of 290 different car makes were on the market. The huge new Motor Speedway at Indianapolis was completed and the first race held.

This 1906 Corbin, with its up-to-date curtains and top, has flared fenders and fins that are far ahead of their time. In fact, styling like this does not come into vogue until the 1950s.

The portable hand pumper gives custom service as an early Packard gets a new supply of gasoline on a city street. During this period gasoline was cheap, but the big problem was general availability. In most large cities it could be obtained from curbside pumps, but the most familiar source in smaller towns and villages was the hardware store. It was purchased in bulk, usually dispensed into an open pan, then carried to the car where it was strained through a chamois and funneled into the tank.

The self-starter was the most talked-about new development of 1912, with the electric version invented by Charles F. Kettering appearing first on the Cadillac. Electric lights, available on many cars, made night-time driving another appealing reason to give up the horse. Painted center lines appeared on highways for the first time.

Interest in the growth of the motion picture industry in the decade almost paralleled that of the automobile. Full-length feature films, such as *Quo Vadis?* in 1913, were coming from Europe. The classic *Birth of a Nation* stirred the imagination with David W. Griffith's innovative closeups, fade-ins and dissolves.

And while Cadillac was promoting its new high-speed V-8 engine and Packard its new twelve which it called the Twin Six, the war was spreading ominously in Europe. It was a distant war to most Americans, but the U.S. automobile industry was gearing up to help the Allies by providing trucks of varied types and designs to haul troops and supplies to the front, as well as staff cars and ambulances.

Across the nation, touring was becoming a national adventure. Planning a trip, no matter the number of miles, was a family affair. Many motorists were learning how to patch tires, which usually would go flat or become punctured at 100 miles or so. They were becoming experts at dodging deep ruts and farm animals that would not budge from the roads that for centuries had been their exclusive domain.

Mark Twain is seated in the back of this powerful 1906 Oldsmobile. The famous writer and humorist autographed the original picture and sent it to Roy D. Chapin, who was sales manager for Oldsmobile. Chapin was one of the founders in 1909 of the Hudson Motor Car Company.

Driving a 1906 Martini runabout is Jacob Ruppert, Jr., possibly remembered more for having built Yankee Stadium in the Bronx than for having managed the Jacob Ruppert brewery for close to half a century, or even for serving as a Democratic congressman from New York from 1899 to 1907. He became president of the New York Yankees baseball club in December 1914 and served until his death in 1939. The Martini, one of the finest of the few products of the motor industry in Switzerland, was built from 1897 to 1933.

MICHIGAN HISTORY DIVISION

President Theodore Roosevelt came to Lansing, Michigan in 1907 to give the principal address on the occasion of the fiftieth anniversary of Michigan Agricultural College (now Michigan State University). He was driven in a 1907 Reo to the campus by Reo Motor Car Company's president, Ransom E. Olds. In the back seat are President Roosevelt (left) and the president of the college. In front are Olds, at the wheel, and Roosevelt's secretary, William Lord.

AMERICAN MOTORS CORPORATION

*William Jennings Bryan, three times an unsuccessful candidate for president of the United States, was at the railroad station in Milwaukee when this picture was taken in 1907. He is shaking hands with the former governor of Wisconsin, George W. Peck, who also authored the **Peck's Bad Boy** book series. Bryan, who championed a belief in the free and unlimited coinage of silver, is in a Rambler, made in nearby Kenosha. Rambler automobiles were produced from 1902 to 1914 when the name was changed to Jeffery. The firm was bought in 1916 by Charles W. Nash, who formed the Nash Motors Company.*

Behind the wheel of this attractive 1907 Packard Thirty runabout is Henry B. Joy, wealthy Detroiter who engineered the transfer of the Packard Motor Car Company to Detroit from Warren, Ohio in 1904. He joined with other investors, including Russell A. Alger, Jr., Joy's passenger in this picture, in buying the firm and moving it into a huge new plant designed by architect Albert Kahn. Joy was Packard's chief executive officer until 1918.

William Howard Taft was a member of President Theodore Roosevelt's cabinet when this picture was taken. He is emerging from a 1907 White steamer at the Oyster Bay station prior to visiting the president at his home in Sagamore Hills. The White was one of the most successful steam cars built in the world, produced in Cleveland by a company that was making sewing machines. White steamers were built from 1901 to 1912. The company made gasoline-powered cars from 1909 to 1922, after which it concentrated on trucks.

Buffalo Bill loved publicity, and one of the easiest ways to get it was to pose in an automobile. Here he sits in a 1908 White steamer.

Here's the intrepid Buffalo Bill again (unmistakable with his Western hat and flowing white hair), this time in a 1908 Rambler.

This rare photograph shows John Mohler Studebaker in a 1908 Studebaker electric victoria-phaeton. He and his brother Clem in 1852 founded a company in South Bend, Indiana to build wagons and carriages. Studebaker began manufacturing automobiles in 1902.

Germany's Kaiser Wilhelm II (seated) is greeted by the Duke of Ratibor during an honor ride of the Imperial Automobile Club, probably in 1908. The car is a Mercedes Cardan, built from 1908 to 1913.

Automotive pioneer H. H. Bassett posed in a 1908 Buick roadster, outside the Weston-Mott plant in Flint, Michigan. Bassett came to Flint with Charles Stewart Mott in 1905, as general manager of Weston-Mott, then a major producer of wheels and axles. In 1920 he became president of Buick, succeeding Walter P. Chrysler (who had succeeded Charles W. Nash).

This photograph of Mark Twain in a 1908 Rambler was taken just two years before his death and thirty-two years after he authored the legendary **Adventures of Tom Sawyer.** The real name of the famed humorist (center, back seat) was, of course, Samuel B. Clemens.

This snappy motorcar of 1908 was called a skimabout by its maker, Palmer-Singer Manufacturing Company of Long Island City, New York. Adorned in the latest fashion including a luxurious fur is a Broadway star whose identity unfortunately is unknown. Cars of that period had 100 per cent visibility, with no windshield and no top.

The great operatic contralto, Ernestine Schumann-Heink, is pictured with her eight children in a 1908 American Berliet, at her home near Montclair, New Jersey. Her husband is standing on the doorstep. This sturdy car was the American version of the French Berliet which subsequently became the Alco, made by the American Locomotive Automobile Company, New York. Madame Schumann-Heink, born near Prague, made her American debut in 1898 in Chicago and sang with the Metropolitan for many years. With a repertoire of 150 roles, she was an extraordinary actress.

Tipping his hat to the crowd is President Theodore Roosevelt, seated in his White steam car in 1908. The only automobile permitted in the Roosevelt inaugural parade of 1905 was a White driven by Walter C. White, who later became president of the company that built the car.

Mary Garden (far left), the great opera singer, is seated in a 1908 Pierce-Arrow. A remarkable woman who ate only one meal a day and remained at 112 pounds all her adult life, she made her debut in 1900 in Charpentier's opera **Louise,** *a role she sang 100 times. She became best known for her role as Mélisande in Debussey's* **Pelléas et Mélisande.** *Mary Garden, who never married, died in her native Aberdeen, Scotland in 1967 at the age of ninety-three. The Pierce-Arrow, one of the most successful luxury cars, also had a long life—from 1900 to 1938.*

One of the alltime great baseball players, Honus Wagner, is seated in a 1909 Regal, made in Detroit from 1907 to 1918. Wagner, a premier shortstop, played with the Pittsburgh Pirates from 1900 to 1917. He was elected to the National Baseball Hall of Fame in 1936.

The speaker of the U.S. House of Representatives, Joseph G. Cannon (center, wearing sailor straw hat), toured Indiana in a new 1909 Overland touring car. From Illinois, Cannon served in Congress from 1873 to 1923, except for two terms, and was speaker from 1903 to 1911. The Overland, one of the most successful American cars, was built for most of its life in Toledo, Ohio. For several years prior to World War I, it ranked second only to Ford in sales.

President William Howard Taft was so huge he needed almost the entire back seat of this 1909 Rambler. The photograph was taken in Augusta, Georgia on November 8, 1909.

Here is another photograph of President William Howard Taft, this time riding in a 1909 Packard Thirty. He is being welcomed in Savannah, Georgia.

25

Three stars of the Detroit Tigers baseball team pose rather somberly in a 1909 Chalmers-Detroit Thirty. (The Thirty indicated the horsepower.) From the left they are Sam Crawford, who later was to be inducted into baseball's Hall of Fame; Germany Schaeffer and Donie Bush, who won the car in a popularity contest. The Chalmers-Detroit, produced in Detroit from 1909-10, became the Chalmers beginning with the 1911 model year.

At the wheel of his racy 1909 Pope-Hartford roadster is Frank Chance, immortalized as the first baseman in baseball's Tinkers-to-Evers-to-Chance doubleplay combination. Chance spent many years with the Chicago Cubs, several of them as manager, but few remember him as the first manager of the New York Yankees, in 1913. The Pope-Hartford, an expensive car, was built in Hartford, Connecticut from 1903 to 1914 by Albert A. Pope.

Braving the cold in a 1910 Brush runabout is Battling Nelson, the Danish-American professional boxer whose real name was Oscar Matthew Nelson. The Brush, built in Detroit from 1907 to 1911, was a low-priced car that featured a wooden axle, which prompted the uncomplimentary slogan, "Wooden axle, wooden body, wouldn't run."

Actress Annette Kellerman poses with a 1910 Buick Model Ten Surrey, all dressed for the theater. She appeared in four silent films produced from 1916 to 1920, including **Queen of the Sea** *in 1918. Buick had an excellent year in 1910, finishing second to Ford by fewer than 2,000 cars.*

Peering out of a 1910 Panhard touring coupe is one of the richest women in the world, the Duchesse de Talleyrand Perigord. She had been Anna Gould, daughter of Jay Gould, the American multi-millionaire financier. The Panhard, one of the great names in automobile history, was built in France from 1889 to 1967.

Certainly Santa Claus must be ranked as one of the most popular personalities of any era. Here, in a 1910 Overland, he entertains a group of Toledo youngsters, all of whom seem unconcerned that the car is parked too close to a fire hydrant.

Behind the wheel of a 1910 Anhut Six toy tonneau is stage and screen actress Florence Auer. The Anhut had a brief life, built by the Anhut Motor Car Company in Detroit from 1909 to 1911.

The noted French comedienne Anna Held, seated in a 1910 Mercer, shades her eyes from the sun. A native of Paris, she made her debut there in 1890. She starred in **The Little Dutchess** at the New York Casino in 1903 and 1904, and in **Miss Innocence** at the New York Theatre in 1909 and 1910. The Mercer, one of the most exciting cars ever built, was named for Mercer County, New Jersey, where it was manufactured from 1909 to 1925. The most famous Mercer was the 1911 raceabout, designed by Finley Robertson Porter.

When the task of rebuilding Abraham Lincoln's home in Springfield, Illinois was completed in 1910, President William Howard Taft came to the Illinois capital for the dedication. He rode in a rare car, a Springfield, made briefly in Springfield, Illinois after the company was transferred from (of all places) Springfield, Massachusetts.

WHITE MOTOR CORPORATION

Reno, Nevada was the site of a historic heavyweight fight on July 4, 1910, as James J. Jeffries came out of retirement to challenge the champion, Jack Johnson. Both fighters are pictured in training, with 1910 White steam cars keeping pace with them. Jeffries, at left, is doing roadwork with his manager, Sam Berger. The great Jack Johnson, at right, kayoed Jeffries in the fifteenth round to hold his crown.

*This rare photograph of Buster Keaton and his younger brother Jingles was taken in a 1910 Browniekar when both were youngsters. Buster was born Joseph Francis Keaton in Piqua, Kansas in 1895. He got his nickname from Harry Houdini, the magician, who admired the way Keaton at the age of six months survived a fall down a flight of stairs at a boardinghouse for stage people. Keaton left the stage, where he was very popular, for supporting roles in films directed by Roscoe "Fatty" Arbuckle. His first picture was **The Butcher Boy**. His initial feature as a star was **The Saphead** in 1920. From this success he went on to become a leading actor, director, producer and screenwriter. Married to Natalie Talmadge in 1921, he appeared in Hollywood films until 1966. One of his last was **A Funny Thing Happened on the Way to the Forum**.*

The Browniekar, a child's gasoline-powered vehicle, was built from 1908 to 1910 by Omar Motor Car Company in a factory in Newark, New York where the Mora automobile had been produced. Its tiny one-cylinder engine permitted a top speed of twelve miles per hour. The car sold for $175.

Tyrus Raymond "Ty" Cobb, considered by many to be the greatest baseball player of all time, bought a 1910 Owen. This Detroit-built car was short-lived, being produced from 1910 to 1912. Cobb starred in the major leagues for twenty-four years. He was with the Detroit Tigers from 1905 to 1926 when he was traded to the Philadelphia Athletics. He was elected to the National Baseball Hall of Fame in 1936.

Buffalo Bill turned up again in Lansing, Michigan in 1910, riding with five other dignitaries in an Oldsmobile. Note the two-level running board and the low-entrance front door. For posterity, occupants are (from the left as you look at them): William Little (Pawnee Bill), Claude H. Winters (the driver), Henry Beheardt, Lansing's chief of police and Buffalo Bill's nephew, Mrs. Little and the buffalo hunter himself.

Earle C. Anthony, Packard distributor for California, is pictured in a 1911 Packard roadster. Probably one of the most effective salesmen the auto industry ever spawned, Anthony was never at a loss to take advantage of an opportunity to sell a Packard automobile. He provided cars for parades, gave red-carpet treatment to dignitaries (who had to travel from the railroad station to their hotels in some kind of car, and it might as well be a Packard), then made sure photographers were on hand to record the event. He hired experts to handle publicity, and constantly had his name before the public in newspapers and on radio.

When this photograph of Woodrow Wilson with his 1911 Cadillac touring car was taken, he was governor of New Jersey. In the following year he would be nominated by the Democratic Party to run for president and would defeat two former presidents, William Howard Taft and Theodore Roosevelt.

One year after purchasing a 1910 Owen car, baseball star Ty Cobb of the Detroit Tigers decided he would rather own this 1911 Chalmers. A successful automobile almost from its beginning in 1910, the Detroit-built Chalmers was a major competitor in the industry for many years. Chalmers merged in 1919 with Maxwell, which became Chrysler Corporation in 1924.

It's President Taft again, this time emerging from a 1911 Oakland into his railroad car at the station in Detroit. The Oakland, made from 1907 to 1931 in Pontiac, Michigan, became part of General Motors in 1909. Contrary to general belief, the Oakland did not become the Pontiac. The GM division introduced the Pontiac in 1928, and for four consecutive model years after that, both Oakland and Pontiac automobiles were marketed.

President William Howard Taft (wearing a top hat, in back seat) showed up in a 1912 Oldsmobile Limited at the dedication in Monroe, Michigan of the Custer Memorial.

Certainly one of the most important personalities in any major city is the fire chief. Here Detroit's chief, W. H. Chittenden, sits proudly behind the wheel of his official car, a 1912 Cartercar. The car was named for Byron J. Carter, who has commanded too little credit for his pioneering in the automobile industry. He began experiments as early as 1887, was a founder in 1902 of the long-lived Jackson Automobile Company in Jackson, Michigan, and is credited with development of the friction-drive principle which gave the Cartercar, produced from 1906 to 1915, its early prominence. The Cartercar Company became part of General Motors in 1909.

Nicholas II, last emperor and czar of Russia (standing left of the hatless man not in uniform), inspects his White Squadron at St. Petersburg in 1912. The trucks pictured are also Whites.

Photographed in Cologne, Germany in a 1913 Mercedes landaulet are the German Imperial Couple, Kaiser Wilhelm and Empress Victoria.

Louis Chevrolet, after whom the car was named, sits behind the wheel of a 1913 Buick touring car. For several years prior to the introduction by William C. Durant of the first Chevrolet car, Louis headed a successful Buick racing team that won national acclaim for the car and the driver.

Thomas A. Edison, the noted inventor and manufacturer of electric batteries, is the passenger in a 1913 Bailey Electric built in Amesbury, Massachusetts. The firm that produced it, S. R. Bailey & Company, was founded in 1856 as a builder of sleighs and carriages. Bailey Electrics, made from 1907 to 1915, did not resemble conventional electrics in appearance, but were distinguished by their smoothly contoured front ends.

The tradition of inviting an automobile manufacturer to provide the pace car for the Indianapolis 500 race began with the first official event in 1911. In three of the first four years (except for 1912), the car was a Stoddard-Dayton, and the driver was Carl G. Fisher, who more than any other man was responsible for building and promoting the Speedway. He was its president for many years. Fisher was also one of the original promoters of Miami Beach in Florida. He is shown pacing the 1913 race in a Stoddard-Dayton, a popular car made in Dayton, Ohio.

The great Scottish entertainer Harry Lauder (wearing a plaid fedora) is seated in a 1913 Hudson touring car. Born in Edinburgh in 1870, he made more than forty American tours beginning in 1906. Lauder was a comedian, a singer and a song writer whose renditions appear on some of the earliest phonograph records made in this country. He authored such perennial favorites as "Roamin' in the Gloamin'" and "It's Nice to Get Up in the Morning." The Hudson automobile was produced in Detroit from 1909 to 1954. After the merger of Hudson and Nash-Kelvinator in 1954, Hudson cars were built in Kenosha, Wisconsin through 1957.

This unique race car was entered in the 1914 Indianapolis 500-mile race by Ettore Bugatti, the great Italian-born designer who built cars in France. Powered by a 390-cubic-inch four-cylinder engine, it finished fifteenth, being forced out of the race on the 134th lap by a broken drive pinion. The car, driven by Ernst Friedrich, was running in second position at 100 miles. It had qualified at 87.73 mph.

With a 1914 Detroit Electric is the brilliant electrical engineer Charles P. Steinmetz. A native of Germany, he was named consulting engineer to General Electric in 1893, a position he held for many years. He authored many technical books on electricity and illumination. The Detroit Electric, most successful of the various electric car makes, was built from 1907 to 1939. Its greatest popularity came in the period from about 1912 to 1923.

Another purchaser of a 1914 Detroit Electric was Thomas A. Edison. Did he ever smile?

*At the wheel of a 1914 Hudson touring car is Alma Gluck, a noted soprano who made her debut with the Metropolitan Opera in 1909 as Sophie in Massenet's **Werther**. Born Reba Fiersohn in Bucharest, Roumania, she gave up opera after three years for the concert stage. Her second husband was violinist Efrem Zimbalist.*

HENRY FORD MUSEUM. THE EDISON INSTITUTE

Three noted Americans who loved nature and camping out were joined by a fourth in making annual motor caravan tours of scenic areas of the United States from 1915 to 1924. With a 1914 Model T Ford, one of several vehicles that made it all possible, are (from the left) John Burroughs, writer and naturalist; Thomas A. Edison, famous inventor, and Henry Ford, the auto magnate. The fourth member of "the vagabonds," as they called themselves, was Harvey Firestone, founder of the Firestone Tire & Rubber Company.

COMMENTARY

They often wore ties and seldom rolled up their white long-sleeve shirts. Most of the time they were attired in three-piece suits and wore hats. But they had wonderful times, these titans of industry who every year from 1915 to 1924 made leisurely motoring tours of selected scenic areas of the United States.

It was a novel adventure that Henry Ford first proposed to Thomas A. Edison, Harvey S. Firestone and John Burroughs back in 1915, as I learned in researching the background of several vehicles in the Henry Ford Museum in 1978 during my four years as curator of transportation. For the "four vagabonds," as they later called themselves, were not going to stay in hotels or motor courts. They were going to camp out.

Camping out then, however, was relatively unknown so the trips had to be carefully planned, and special vehicles had to be developed to make the ventures successful. The vagabonds did not know it, of course, but they were pioneers in what became the recreational vehicle industry.

Beginning in 1915 and lasting until 1924, the annual odysseys took the president of Ford Motor Company, the president of the Firestone Tire & Rubber Company, the internationally known inventor and the noted naturalist and writer to such areas as the Blue Ridge Mountains, the Adirondacks, New England and Northern Michigan. On one trip, they were joined by the president of the United States, Warren G. Harding,

accompanied by the usual Secret Service contingent.

While the distinguished travelers slept on cots under tents, they did not cook their own meals over open fires. Their servants prepared food with portable stoves and served the meals on a large round table that could be disassembled.

Several trucks were used to haul the equipment and supplies. A small fleet of automobiles (not always limited to Ford-built cars) carried the travelers, as well as the servants who brought the pleasures of home living to the woods and streams. They traveled slowly in a long convoy.

Three vehicles used on the trips have survived and are exhibited in the Ford Museum. One is a refrigeration truck converted from what had been a Lincoln limousine. It served as the camp kitchen since it included a compartment for storage of ice, as well as space for tools and utensils. The second is a large White truck that hauled heavy equipment and supplies. The third vehicle is a Ford truck that was used, after 1918, to haul water. The body was constructed of sheet metal over wood with the interior containing a large water tank as well as drawers and storage area for kitchen utensils.

The vagabonds discontinued their annual sojourns after Burroughs became incapacitated because of age, and their excursions attracted too much public attention.

A cold snowy day in New York did not concern Ann Pennington, Broadway and film star who owned this 1915 Ohio Electric which could easily be started in any kind of weather. Star of the Ziegfeld Follies and George White's Scandals, she soon was to appear in her first movie, **Susie Snowflake**. The Ohio Electric was produced in Toledo from 1909 to 1918.

The original of this picture, taken by Brown Brothers, indicated that President Woodrow Wilson (far left) was "with a party at Sea Girt, New Jersey, in a 1915 Lozier." A well-made expensive car, the Lozier was made originally in Plattsburg, New York, from 1905 to 1910, when the company moved to Detroit. It lasted until 1917.

Mabel Normand, who appeared in eleven silent films with Charlie Chaplin, sits proudly behind the wheel of her 1915 Stutz touring car. At fifteen she worked as a model for the artist, James Montgomery Flagg. She started in films with Biograph in 1909. Mack Sennett in 1912 took her with him to Keystone Film Company to make a series of split-film slapstick comedies at studios he developed at Elendale, California. She is said to have been the first movie personality to throw a custard pie at anyone. The Stutz, built in Indianapolis from 1912 to 1935, was an excellent car in the medium and high-priced range, designed by Harry C. Stutz.

"She reigned supreme as 'America's Sweetheart' in the era of silent films," the **New York Times** observed when Mary Pickford died in 1979 at the age of eighty-six. The famous Canadian-born actress is shown here with a 1915 Maxwell roadster. She entered films at fifteen and became a star with **The Poor Little Rich Girl** in 1917. Other famous Pickford pictures were **Daddy Longlegs, Pollyanna** and **Little Lord Fauntleroy.** She retired in 1932. The Maxwell was one of America's most popular cars for more than two decades. It started out in Tarrytown, New York in 1904. The company was moved in 1913 to Detroit and eventually became part of Chrysler Corporation.

Actress Billie Burke is pictured in a 1915 Studebaker Six tourer in San Francisco's Golden Gate Park. "A delicate beauty of piquant personality" is how one film critic described her. She was born in Washington, D.C. and spent her childhood in London. She returned to New York in 1907 to star opposite John Drew in the stage play **My Wife.** Miss Burke married Florenz Ziegfeld in 1914 and starred in numerous films and plays before her death in 1970 at eighty-five.

1916-1925: *A New Freedom*

It was a decade born in turmoil that spawned a president who made normalcy out of normality, a time of prohibition, of fears that a Bolshevik lurked in every alley, of bobbed hair, stucco houses and jazz. The farmer came to town more often because chances are now he owned a Model T Ford. Movie theaters were everywhere. Newspapers sold for two cents daily, ten cents on Sundays, and everybody read the funnies. It was a time of new freedom for women, of ice-cream cones and hot dogs.

And the automobile shared in all of it. Suburbs mushroomed outside America's major cities, and while many breadwinners took the train to work, more and more of them used private passenger cars. Motor trucks, too, took on new roles. They delivered groceries, picked up laundry and hawked fresh fruits and vegetables door to door. Not many were hauling heavy goods and supplies from one city to another because the roads in America were still terrible. In fact, in many areas there were no roads at all.

A sign of hope was the first Federal law, signed by President Wilson in July 1916, aimed at establishing a nationwide system of interstate highways. The first road, less than three

MVMA

Many cities in the early 1920s passed ordinances prohibiting the dispensing of gasoline near buildings of any kind. Curbside pumps were most often used. In many cases it took two men to do the job — one to hold the hose and the other to operate the manual pump. Usually the hapless motorist hadn't the faintest idea of whether he got the exact number of gallons he paid for. Visible pumps did not come until later.

miles in length, was completed in January 1918. By the end of 1920 only 191 miles of Federal-aid highways had been constructed in the entire country.

While they waited, Americans took to what roads there were. It was a time of detours, either for local construction or repairs, or because rains or floods had washed out road sections or bridges. A new American phenomenon, the travel court, appeared along some highways. In the beginning most were unheated and had no electric lights. Burma Shave drew smiles with its humorous rows of roadside signs. More likely than not, many car owners were just "out for a ride," although some adventurous souls chanced longer journeys to visit relatives.

Almost all automobiles built in the decade 1916 to 1925 had cloth tops. It was not that motorists did not have the choice of buying closed cars. They were much more expensive than open models — and, besides, it was easy to put up a top, as this young lady is demonstrating with her 1920 National car.

War was raging in Europe as the decade began, and within a year America joined the conflict. All car and truck manufacturers offered their full co-operation to the Government, but production of passenger cars was not suspended. In addition to trucks and military vehicles, the industry turned out shells, helmets, caissons, aircraft engines, tractors, tanks, naval craft, antiaircraft guns and gun

carriages. In 1918 shortages of coal and petroleum developed, causing heatless days and gasless Sundays.

When the armistice finally came in November, the doughboys returned home to find an America awakened to opportunities for a new and better way of life. Much of that new spirit came from the freedom brought to the American family by the automobile, which in a few years would become less of a luxury and more of a necessity, within easier reach of more and more families.

The fabulous success of the Model T Ford had much to do with the new directions the industry was beginning to take. Ford Motor Company continued to expand its factories, taking advantage of every opportunity to increase production and trim costs. By keeping the same basic engine and transmission year after year, with only minor changes in chassis and body designs, the Model T eventually got low enough in price that families that never before had even considered owning cars were in a position to buy them. The many Ford moves to broaden its market fathered new competition. Chevrolet in this period was feeling its way, and such relative newcomers as Essex and Star became strong contenders for a bigger share of the low-priced field.

All kinds of solutions to America's crying need to build substantial roads and highways were attempted. A 1917 Ford tries out this plank road under construction somewhere in the West.

The manufacture of bodies for closed cars in this period called for the skills of cabinet makers. Here is a scene in the Packard plant where much of the body was fashioned of wood.

When the decade began, ten per cent of all cars being produced were closed models. As the automobile became more and more of a year-around vehicle, the appeal of the open car began to wane. But it was not until the price of the closed car came closer to that of the cheaper touring car that the trend took on momentum. Alfred P. Sloan in his book *My Years With General Motors* credits the introduction by Hudson Motor Car Company in 1922 of the Essex coach with starting it all. It was a new body style (now called a two-door sedan), and the price was closer than ever to that of the lowest-priced open model. So dramatic were the subsequent results — with other manufacturers introducing similar coach models — that by 1925 more than half the cars shown at the National Automobile Show were closed models.

Passenger car sales passed the four million mark in 1923 for the first time, and half of them were Model T Fords. But even Model T owners were beginning to wonder when Henry Ford was going to bring out a more modern car. The forces of competition were determinedly at work, and the automobile was soon to take on a new personality.

Wilbert Robinson, manager of the Brooklyn Dodgers baseball team, poses proudly in his sleek new 1916 Roamer. After an active career as a catcher from 1886 to 1902, Robinson managed the Brooklyn team from 1914 to 1931. He was inducted into baseball's Hall of Fame in 1945. The Roamer automobile was built in Kalamazoo, Michigan from 1916 to 1930 by the Barley Motor Company. Later models were deliberate copies of the Rolls-Royce design.

Identities of these two lovely young ladies, both probably budding stage or screen actresses, are unknown to the author. They are enjoying a ride in a 1916 Maxwell, with a special custom body and jaunty victoria top.

Before he became a national hero as an airplane pilot in World War I, Eddie Rickenbacker was a celebrated race driver on the dirt and board tracks across America. Here he is at the wheel of a 1916 Maxwell racer at the Indianapolis Motor Speedway.

Standing beside a 1916 Jeffery Quad truck is General John J. Pershing, who would command the American Expeditionary Force sent to France a year later. The Quad was a successful four-wheel-drive and four-wheel-steer vehicle developed by the Thomas B. Jeffery Company of Kenosha, Wisconsin. Following the purchase of the Jeffery firm by Charles W. Nash in late summer of 1916, the truck became the Nash Quad. Thousands saw service in World War I.

Indianapolis was the home of many fine cars in the early days of the automobile industry. One was the Cole, built from 1909 to 1925 by a company that had established a national reputation for building horsedrawn carriages. Its president, J. J. Cole, is at the wheel of this 1916 Cole Model 860G, taken in University Park, Indianapolis. The company discontinued car production in 1925, not because sales were faltering but because its owners felt the market might decline and the time was right to liquidate.

45

*Going for a ride in the park with her 1916 Packard Twin Six touring car and her dog is the internationally renowned Russian ballet dancer, Anna Pavlova. She made her American debut on February 28, 1910, at the Metropolitan as Swanilda in **Coppélia.** She left Russia in 1914 to live in London. With her own company, she toured most of the world. As a biographer observed in 1959: "Even today, her name is not only a legend but an inspiration to the young. Children are still learning because their mothers saw Pavlova years ago."*

*Anna Held, the comedienne seen earlier with a 1910 Mercer, had this 1916 Packard Twin-Six limousine custom finished. It is painted a milk white. Note the rear wheel spokes are different in design from those in front. Miss Held appeared in her only motion picture in 1916, **Madame la Presidente.***

Great Britain's King George V (center) has just finished a tour of the battlefields in 1917. Field Marshal Earl Hay is at his right. A Rolls-Royce town car awaits them. The king reigned from 1910 to 1936.

46

In the summer of 1917, when this picture was taken, Eddie Rickenbacker was the official chauffeur to General John J. Pershing, commander in chief of the American forces in France. His car is a Hudson Super-Six phaeton. Rickenbacker (who went on to become America's top air ace during World War I), was an investor in an automobile company bearing his name and became chief executive of Eastern Airlines. He is greeting Arthur Duray, then in the French army, who in 1913 set an automobile speed record at Ostend of 142.9 mph. At right is Jean Chassgne, holder of the two-mile record of 118.9 mph at Brooklands.

The talented Pathé child film star Baby Marie Osborne was earning $1,000 a week in 1917, when this picture was taken of her leaving for the studio in her own chauffeur-driven Hudson sedan.

Fridtjof Nansen, the distinguished Norwegian explorer, scientist, statesman and humanitarian, is the driver of this 1917 Hudson Super-Six phaeton. In 1922 he received a Nobel Peace Prize.

Mischa Elman, the noted violinist, owned this 1917 Hudson Super-Six phaeton. A native of Russia, he was welcomed as a great artist in St. Petersburg in 1904 when he was only thirteen. He won acclaim in America during six concert tours.

*The swashbuckling star of the silent screen, Douglas Fairbanks, loved to practice his stunts almost anywhere, including on top of the gasoline tank of his 1917 Mercer runabout. Born Douglas Ullman in 1883, he was an acrobatic, ever-smiling hero of many comedies and costume adventures, almost all of which he produced himself. His popular films included **The Half Breed** in 1916, **The Mark of Zorro** in 1920, **The Three Musketeers** in 1921 and **The Thief of Baghdad** in 1923. He was Mary Pickford's first husband. Fairbanks died in 1939 at fifty-six.*

*Vitagraph stars Edith Storey and Antonio Moreno are pictured with a 1917 Hupmobile roadster outside their film studio. Moreno, owner of the car, appeared in many motion pictures for several decades. Miss Storey starred in **Enemy to the King** made in 1916. The popular Hupmobile had a long and successful life. It was built in Detroit from 1908 to 1940. Its last venture was the Hupp Skylark, produced with the dies of the defunct Cord.*

With four stars on its radiator, the official car of General John J. Pershing when he arrived in France in 1917 was a Cadillac. The commander in chief of the American Expeditionary Forces is preparing to review his troops.

Baseball umpire Frank "Silk" O'Loughlin, who looked more like a wealthy banker, bought this 1917 Chalmers touring car with its flashy wire wheels. He umpired in the American League for many years.

In a 1917 Maxwell cabriolet that seems almost as high as it is long is actress Hazel Dawn, who appeared in only two motion pictures, each thirty years apart. She was in **Under Cover** in 1916 and **Margie** in 1946.

Billie Rhodes was filming the comedy **Some Nurse** for Strand-Mutual when this picture of her in a 1917 Scripps-Booth roadster was taken. She was the popular star of Al Christie comedies and other short films beginning in 1911. They included **Perils of the Sea** in 1913 and **Girl of My Dreams** in 1918. The distinctive Scripps-Booth car was built in Detroit from 1914 to 1922.

*Edward S. "Ned" Jordan sits behind the wheel of a 1918 Jordan sport roadster. A pioneer in the automobile industry, he is best remembered for changing the entire course of car advertising, emphasizing, as he put it years later, "the sizzle instead of the steak." His most memorable ad, for the legendary Jordan Playboy, titled "Somewhere West of Laramie," appeared in the **Saturday Evening Post** on June 23, 1923. Before forming his own company in Cleveland in 1916, Jordan had been sales manager in Kenosha, Wisconsin of the Thomas B. Jeffery Company which built the original Rambler car.*

COMMENTARY

Twenty years after the last Jordan car was built, Ned Jordan began writing a column of nostalgia for *Automotive News*, the weekly magazine read by more automotive people than any other publication. Nash Motors had just announced it planned to revive the Rambler name in introducing a new series of smaller cars in the spring of 1950. Jordan lauded the move in one of his columns and recounted how he had once been sales manager for Thomas B. Jeffery Company of Kenosha, Wisconsin, which built the original Rambler from 1902 to 1914.

Following publication of that column, I wrote a long letter to Jordan, then associated with McArthur Advertising Corporation in New York which produced posters for subway and railroad cars. I expressed the hope that he had saved original catalogs, correspondence, photographs and other material from his Jeffery days that he might be willing to contribute to Nash-Kelvinator's archives. In three days back came an equally long letter from Jordan thanking me for sending Nash and Rambler historical material I thought he would like to have and apologizing for not having saved a thing of value from his automobile days.

He explained how he got the job with Rambler: "About August 1, 1907, having been fired by John H. Patterson of National Cash Register, I met Charlie Jeffery at the station, had lunch in the diner and was hired as advertising manager. I was successively branch manager, sales manager and secretary of the Jeffery company before I was thirty. Confidentially, I was the one who encouraged Charlie to sell to Nash, because he knew I was then planning to organize the Jordan Company in January 1916."

Jordan and I corresponded intermittently for about a year after that. On one occasion he sent me an autographed copy of his famous little privately-printed book, *The Story of Adam and Eve*. I saved that, but unfortunately only a few letters.

Nash Motors was founded in 1916, after Charles W. Nash resigned as president of General Motors to start a company under his own name. However, because he took over a going concern in Kenosha, Wisconsin that was still producing Jeffery cars and trucks, Nash after World War II began advertising it built "great cars since 1902," tracing its ancestry to the initial one-cylinder Rambler runabout first offered for public sale in March 1902. (Charles Nash relinquished managerial control of the company in 1937 following the merger with Kelvinator, but he had always insisted that no reference ever be made to the company's ancestry. As far as he was concerned, the company began in 1916 — and sales, advertising and publicity staffs were instructed not to refer to what happened before that date.)

It followed, however, that in 1952 Nash would be in a

position to celebrate its fiftieth anniversary. The Nash-Kelvinator public relations staff as well as the advertising department planned all kinds of activities and promotions to call attention to the observance. We sponsored a "search your attic" campaign in Kenosha and offered modest prizes for the best original Rambler material, much of which eventually became part of the company's historical collection. A highlight of the celebration was to be a civic banquet in Kenosha in the spring of 1952. I suggested that we invite the fifty oldest Nash employees from the standpoint of length of service to be our special guests. We planned also to invite the governor of Wisconsin, top UAW officials and key business and industry leaders of the Kenosha and Milwaukee areas. The question soon arose: who would be the master of ceremonies? I suggested Ned Jordan, not only because of his early association with the Jeffery company but also because he was an

accomplished speaker with a keen wit. Fred Black, public relations director, agreed, and an invitation was promptly dispatched.

Jordan was delighted. He had not been in southern Wisconsin for years, and he knew there were still a few Kenoshans alive who would remember him. When Edwin R. Moore, Jr., our public relations man in Kenosha, and I met him at the railroad station, we were agreeably surprised to see that he was a vigorous, ruddy-faced, handsome man. He responded to all queries about the past with enthusiasm, and later he was a real hit with Nash-Kelvinator executives, especially George W. Mason, president and chairman, who chatted with Jordan for half an hour before the banquet ceremonies began. I remember that Jordan took the time to shake hands with each of the fifty Nash employee guests including the oldest, Herbert W. Devine, who had started with Jeffery in its first production year, 1902.

Charlie Chaplin, standing by a 1918 King Eight touring car, was an outstanding actor, director, writer and producer in the motion picture industry. When he died in 1977 at the age of eighty-eight, the **New York Times** *called Chaplin "the poignant little tramp with the cane and comic walk who almost single-handedly elevated the novelty entertainment medium of motion pictures into art." He made more than eighty movies between 1914 and 1977. The King, founded by pioneer Charles B. King in Detroit in 1910, lasted until 1924.*

DETROIT PUBLIC LIBRARY

DETROIT PUBLIC LIBRARY

It's Memorial Day, 1919, and the car pacing the Indianapolis 500 race is a Packard Twin Six roadster, driven by Colonel J. G. Vincent, the celebrated Packard engineer who developed the company's twelve-cylinder engine (called a Twin Six from 1915 through 1932). His passenger, looking back at the oncoming race cars, is Eddie Rickenbacker.

Shown with his 1919 Packard Twin Six roadster is the noted Hollywood writer, *Gouverneur Morris*, whose new screen play, **The Penalty,** has just won acclaim. This photograph was taken in 1920 during filming of a new picture, **The Water Lily,** which he also authored.

One of the greatest voices in the history of opera belonged to Enrico Caruso, shown here about to enter a 1920 Hudson limousine in Montreal. The immortal tenor, born in Naples in 1873, sang in most major cities of Europe and America. He made his Metropolitan Opera debut on November 23, 1903. He died in Florence, Italy in 1921 at the young age of forty-eight.

Many readers may never have heard of the Revere, but more than 2,700 were produced in a small factory at Logansport, Indiana from 1917 to 1926. Virtually all were luxury models, including a formal sedan built for Spain's King Alfonso XIII. Most early Reveres were powered by a Rochester-Duesenberg racing engine that developed 103 hp. In this 1920 ReVere (spelled with a capital V beginning in that year), Newton Van Zanat, president, is at the wheel. Seated in back with the woman on his lap is the treasurer, C. H. Wilson.

One of Hollywood's most famous cars in the silent days was the 1920 Pierce-Arrow with a custom body by Don Lee that was built for Roscoe C. "Fatty" Arbuckle, the famed comedian. The photo at left shows him and the car near his home, and at right is a still from one of his many films. Arbuckle was born in Smith Center, Kansas, in 1887, and died in 1933. He began his screen career in 1913 as an extra, later playing leads. Among his classic motion pictures were **Good Night Nurse, The Life of the Party, The Waiter's Ball, The Butcher Boy** *and* **Out West.**

In the 1920s, owners kept luxury cars much longer than they do today. Here California Governor Friend W. Richardson poses with his 1920 Packard Twin Six touring car. The photograph was taken in 1926.

British golfers Harry Vardon and Ted Ray sit in the 1920 Haynes special speedster they used during a tour of the United States. Ray had just won at Inverness at Toledo, Ohio, finishing one stroke ahead of Vardon. Winner of the British Open six times from 1896 to 1914, Vardon won sixty-two first-class championships during his long career. The Haynes, founded in Kokomo, Indiana in 1904 by automotive pioneer Elwood Haynes, lasted until 1925.

MVMA

President Calvin Coolidge has just alighted from the official 1921 Pierce-Arrow seven-passenger sedan used by the White House. An ordinary citizen, if he had $9,000, could buy one just like it. While the car is of 1921 vintage, the picture was taken after Coolidge succeeded Warren G. Harding following the latter's death in office in August, 1923.

MVMA

Stepping out of her 1921 Packard limousine is film actress Louise Fazenda. She made her first motion picture in 1913 for Universal where she developed into an eccentric comedienne in the studio's "Joker" shorts. She joined Mack Sennett's Keystone Films in 1915, and became particularly adept at portraying rural types. She was married to producer Hal. B. Wallis.

DETROIT PUBLIC LIBRARY

Both the car and the personality with it were big and powerful. Riding in a 1921 McFarlan is Jack Dempsey, the world heavyweight boxing champion. The McFarlan was built in Connersville, Indiana from 1910 to 1928. Dempsey was champion from 1919 to 1926. He kayoed Jess Willard in the fourth round in a historic battle in Toledo on July 4, 1919, to win the crown, and lost it to Gene Tunney in 1926.

*Silent film actors Ben Turpin and Madge Bellamy stand beside another 1921 McFarlan, this time a huge town car. Turpin made his first films in 1907. He played with Charlie Chaplin in a 1915 picture, but it was not until he joined Mack Sennett in 1917 that he became a leading comedy star. Among his many films were **Uncle Tom Without the Cabin** in 1919 and **A Harem Knight** in 1926. Madge Bellamy was born Margaret Philpott in 1900. As a screen actress she projected sweet innocence. She starred in **Lorna Doone** in 1922 and **The Iron Horse** in 1924.*

*Many Hollywood stars owned attractive Leach cars built in Los Angeles from 1918 to 1922, in the old Republic truck plant. They were expensive automobiles selling for $5,000 or more. A Leach owner was Betty Blythe, shown with a 1921 touring model that featured the so-called California combination top. Miss Blythe made her film debut in 1918 with Vitagraph in Brooklyn, New York. She played the title role in **Queen of Sheba** when this photo was taken. Among her later films were **Tom Brown of Culver** in 1932, **A Girl of the Limberlost** in 1934 and **Where Are Your Children?** in 1944.*

Another prominent Leach owner was the legendary cowboy film star Tom Mix, shown here with a 1921 chummy roadster in front of his Hollywood home. A United States marshal who turned actor, he starred in more than 400 low-budget westerns. Among scores of Tom Mix thrillers the author remembers are **A Horseman of the Plains** *in 1928 and* **Destry Rides Again** *in 1932.*

Newly-elected President Warren G. Harding waves from the official presidential car, a 1921 Packard phaeton. The photograph was taken April 19, 1921, when the president traveled to New York City for the unveiling of the Bolivar statue. Note the photographers with their cumbersome box cameras.

Harry C. Stutz, driving an H.C.S. roadster, stands ready to pace the 1921 Indianapolis 500 race. He founded the Stutz Motor Car Company in Indianapolis in 1912, establishing a reputation for building distinctive cars of outstanding performance. The firm was reorganized in 1919, and Stutz left to form another company using his initials. The H.C.S. was produced from late in 1919 to 1926.

*In this picture, from the Ford Archives, two Pathé film players are shown on a residential street in Hollywood. In the 1921 Ford at left is actress Kitty O'Day. Behind, stepping out of a 1922 Lincoln touring car, is Douglas MacLean, who starred in numerous light silent movies, many of which he produced himself. One, filmed in 1922, was **The Hottentot**. In the same year Henry Ford purchased the Lincoln Motor Company from Henry M. Leland, who had formed the company two years earlier in Detroit to build high-quality expensive cars.*

One of the great actresses of Hollywood's silent era, Pola Negri, is shown with a 1922 Cadillac seven-passenger sedan. She was born in 1894 in Janowa, Poland, as Barbara Apollonia Chalupiec. She came to Hollywood following a successful career in German films. One biographer called her "a reigning queen of Hollywood, admired for the earthy, passionate, exotic quality of her screen personality." She made two pictures in 1922, **The Last Payment** *and* **The Red Peacock.**

E. G. "Cannon Ball" Baker is at the wheel of the Frontenac which he drove in the 1922 Indianapolis 500. The Frontenac automobile, designed by Louis Chevrolet, who also was president of the firm that built it, had a short life. By 1924, the Indianapolis company was bankrupt. Baker went on to establish a reputation throughout the auto industry as an indefatigable endurance and test driver who established numerous records for such makes as Cadillac, Franklin, Revere, Nash, Oldsmobile, Stutz, Rickenbacker, Whippet, Hudson and Kaiser.

INDIANAPOLIS MOTOR SPEEDWAY

Golfer Gene Sarazen smiles from behind the wheel of his 1922 Packard Single Six roadster. He had many reasons to smile, for in 1922 he not only was U.S. open champion but he also won the PGA tournament that year (as well as in 1923 and 1933). As a matter of interest, the car parked at the left of the Packard is a Stephens Salient Six.

Alton G. Seiberling, vice-president and general manager of the Haynes Automobile Company of Kokomo, Indiana, shows off the new 1922 Haynes 75 special speedster at Broadacres, his palatial country home. Elwood Haynes, the company's founder, built his first car in 1894. He joined with the Apperson Brothers to build the Haynes-Apperson, from 1898 to 1904. The Haynes car was produced from 1904 to 1925.

James Anthony Murphy, champion race driver who won the 1922 Indianapolis 500, stands beside his new 1923 Marmon four-passenger sport speedster. At the time Murphy could boast that he was the only American who had ever won the French Grand Prix race classic. The Marmon, one of the best American cars ever produced, was built in Indianapolis from 1902 to 1933. One of its last offerings was a magnificent V-16 designed by Walter Dorwin Teague.

Helen Lynch and George Fisher use a 1923 Durant roadster to lean on during filming of a picture for J. G. Mayer Productions. Miss Lynch starred in **The Eternal Three** in 1923, and appeared in several gangster pictures in the late 1920s. Fisher was in only three pictures, one as late as 1951.

David Lloyd George, Great Britain's prime minister from 1916 to 1922, holds a wreath in his left hand and seems to be appealing to someone to tell him what to do with it. A 1923 Lincoln touring car draped with American flags is behind him.

This luxurious 1923 Packard Twin Six sedan limousine is a car that Tarzan built. Photographed at Tarzana Ranch are the daughter Joan (left) and the wife of Edgar Rice Burroughs, who made a fortune with his Tarzan books and motion pictures.

They called Ralph DePalma, shown here in a Packard race car at the 1923 Indianapolis 500, "King of the Roaring Road." Certainly one of the greatest pioneer race drivers of all time, he test-drove hundreds of different cars for scores of manufacturers prior to World War I. He won the Indianapolis 500 in 1915, driving a Mercedes.

His trademarks were a waxed moustache and an impeccable wardrobe. Adolphe Menjou, the noted actor of both silent and talking pictures, is behind the wheel of a 1924 Cadillac phaeton. The Pittsburgh-born Menjou in 1923 gained prominence as the suave star of Charlie Chaplin's **A Woman of Paris.** He appeared in many films, and in 1931 was nominated by the Academy of Motion Picture Arts and Sciences for best actor in **The Front Page.**

The Prince of Wales visited the Ford plant in Dearborn, Michigan in 1924. He is pictured in the back seat of a Lincoln touring car with Edsel and Henry Ford, as curious workmen look on. The photograph was taken October 14, 1924.

America's first woman to be elected governor, Miriam A. "Ma" Ferguson of Texas, bought a new Packard soon after her election in 1924. While she is the principal in this picture (standing second from left, next to her daughter Darrin), one might think that distinction belonged to the well-dressed man with hair parted in the middle. But he was only the salesman, O. L. Jones.

Walter P. Chrysler stands beside the first car to bear his name, a 1924 sedan. Formerly the head of Buick and Willys-Overland, he acquired Maxwell-Chalmers in 1923 and almost overnight became one of the most vigorous competitors in the automobile industry. The first Chrysler cars were immediate successes and helped establish for the company a reputation for innovative engineering.

63

Cecil B. DeMille, the great Hollywood producer, loved automobiles, especially this 1924 Cunningham with its balloon tires and sod pans (in place of running boards — his right foot rests on one.) The car was manufactured by James Cunningham, Son & Company, Rochester, New York, a pioneer carriage builder that turned out custom-designed automobiles in limited numbers from 1909 to 1931.

Also the owner of a handsome 1924 Cunningham is Amelita Galli-Curci, the brilliant Italian-American coloratura soprano, shown in a roadster model with her husband. She sang with the Chicago Opera Company from 1916 to 1926 and the Metropolitan from 1921 to 1930, when she left opera for the concert stage.

*The greatest heart-throb of silent films was Rudolph Valentino, shown here with a 1924 Voisin. He starred in thirteen movies from 1921 to 1926, and at the time this photograph was taken was filming the classic **Monsieur Beaucaire**. When he died August 23, 1926, at thirty-one, he was mourned by millions. The Voisin was made in France from 1919 to 1939 by Gabriel Voisin, an early aviation pioneer. Many of his early automobiles were powered by Knight sleeve-valve engines.*

Leaning on the fender of this 1924 Kissel tourster is William S. Hart, the famed silent film star who was a director as well as an actor. He concentrated on realism in a number of classic Western films. Hat in hand and owner of the car is James Montgomery Flagg, the illustrator of versatility and technical skill. He designed forty-five military posters for World War I, including the memorable one showing Uncle Sam pointing directly at the viewer. Between Flagg and Hart is W. H. Wurzburger. The distinctive Kissel was built in Hartford, Wisconsin from 1906 to 1931.

Getting into his new 1924 Flint Six touring car is Beniamino Gigli, famous Italian-born opera star. He sang throughout Europe and South and Central America before joining the Metropolitan Opera in 1920. The tenor appeared in films in Hollywood and Europe from 1937 to 1953. The Flint, built in Elizabeth, New Jersey and Flint, Michigan by one of William C. Durant's companies, was popular from its introduction in 1924 to 1927. More than 39,000 were produced.

William C. Durant (right), founder of General Motors, stands beside a 1924 Durant Model E-55, made by a new company he formed after his ouster as head of the nation's biggest automobile company. The picture was taken in Durant's Asbury, New Jersey showroom. The same building years earlier housed a display room for Durant-Dort carriages.

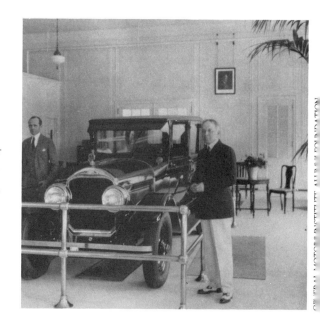

HENRY AUSTIN CLARK COLLECTION

To help promote the Rickenbacker Six automobile, E. G. "Cannon Ball" Baker was engaged as chief test pilot. He set all types of endurance and speed records in many sections of the country. He is behind the wheel, with Eddie Rickenbacker, vice-president of the Rickenbacker Motor Company, standing beside the touring model. The Rickenbacker was built in Detroit from 1922 to 1927.

The official pace car for the 1925 Indianapolis 500-mile race was a Rickenbacker Vertical Eight. It was driven by the World War I ace himself, Eddie Rickenbacker, shown at the wheel. Even though Rickenbacker car production was halted in 1927, as late as 1931 parts were being sold in Flint, Michigan, where the last vestiges of the company had been moved.

CADILLAC MOTOR CAR DIVISION

Glenn H. Curtiss, the inventor and aviator, stands by his 1925 Cadillac five-passenger brougham. His accomplishments are many. He began making Curtiss motorcycles in Hammondsport, New York in 1902, and set numerous speed records with his own models. He designed aeronautical engines for dirigibles and built the first successful hydroplane in 1908. Curtiss also built the "America," the first multi-engined flying boat. He was born in 1878 and died in 1930.

Connecticut's Governor John H. Trumbull, pictured with his official Packard Eight sedan outside the governor's mansion in Hartford, was no exception to the unwritten law of 1925 that all men of consequence wore straw hats in summer.

DETROIT PUBLIC LIBRARY

The Wills Sainte Claire. The car was as impressive as its classic-sounding name. Built in Marysville, Michigan from 1921 to 1926, it was an automobile that many said was too good for its modest price. It was designed by Childe Harold Wills, who had been a close associate of Henry Ford and is credited with much of the work involved in designing the Model T. Wills was insistent on maximum product quality and would often order the production line shut down to correct minor problems. Pictured here is a 1925 Wills Sante Claire roadster, driven by Grace Briggs, daughter of Walter O. Briggs, Detroit industrialist and owner of the Detroit Tigers baseball team

Silent film star Leatrice Joy, seen here in her 1925 chauffeur-driven Packard Eight sedan, is credited with popularizing bobbed hair. Born Leatrice Joy Zeidler in 1896 in New Orleans, she made her debut in Hollywood as an extra in 1915. She became a leading lady in comedies of Billy West and Oliver Hardy and starred in many Cecil B. DeMille silent pictures. In 1925 she appeared in **The Dressmaker from Paris, Hell's High Road** *and* **The Wedding Song.** *Her first husband was matinee idol John Gilbert.*

Advertising executive and artist John E. Sheridan is seated in his 1925 Packard Six convertible coupe with a special custom body he helped design which was built by Rollston. Sheridan, famous for his World War I posters, was a partner in the New York advertising agency of Sheridan & Sheridan.

Standing by his 1925 Packard Eight limousine is the noted illustrator, Harley Ennis Stivers. The photograph was taken by Nick Lazarnick of New York, who unquestionably recorded more automotive history with a camera than anyone else. His massive collection of photographs, beginning with those taken at auto shows at the turn of the century, is part of the National Automotive Collection of the Detroit Public Library.

Actress Dorothy Mackail sits grandly in a 1925 Hispano-Suiza. A former London show girl and Ziegfeld chorine, she played breezy leads in numerous Hollywood silent films and early talking pictures. Two of them were **His Children's Children** *in 1923 and* **The Reckless Hour** *in 1931. The Hispano-Suiza, one of the great classic cars, was built in Barcelona, Spain from 1904 to 1944, and in France from 1911 to 1938. Miss Mackail's car has a custom body by Kellner.*

Whether she tired of the big Packard she bought in 1924 or whether she wanted another car to run around in is not known, but in 1925 Texas Governor Miriam "Ma" Ferguson purchased this attractive Moon roadster. The Moon was built in St. Louis for more than a quarter century, from 1905 to 1930. It joined scores of other smaller companies in failing during the economic depression of the 1930s.

At the wheel of a 1925 Packard Eight touring car is Al Christie, successful producer of Nestor silent film comedies. He was recognized as a close competitor of Mack Sennett.

A versatile actress, Elinor Boardman, poses with a 1925 Velie club phaeton. She became nationally known as the Kodak Girl on Eastman Kodak publicity posters. Miss Boardman made six films in 1925, but she is best remembered for her leading role in **The Crowd,** directed in 1928 by King Vidor, whom she married and later divorced. Other noted Boardman pictures were **Tell It to the Marines** in 1926 and **Redemption** in 1930. The Velie was made in Moline, Illinois from 1908 to 1929.

1926-1935: *Of Classics and Depression*

The decade which began in 1926 was one filled with promise for the burgeoning automobile industry. There seemed to be a market for almost any kind of car — from the legendary four-cylinder Model T Ford in its second to last year, to the luxurious Pierce-Arrow with its powerful eight-cylinder engine. In 1929 more than five million passenger cars were produced, a record that would stand for twenty years. A year later the handsome little American Austin would appear, at the same time as the Cadillac with a V-16. While powerful, more luxurious automobiles drew appreciative crowds to automobile shows from coast to coast, equal interest

How glorious it was, in 1926, to pull onto a spanking new highway built of smooth cement! It didn't matter if there were no center line, or that the road was narrow, or that the shoulder scarcely permitted a vehicle to pull off for a tire change. It was a concrete highway, and the car could make it to the next town.

A New York salon showing of 1933 Packard open models, many with custom bodies, emphasizes the elegance that was brought to car design in this period. At the lower left is an early Packard Twin Six, exhibited to show the dramatic contrast in appearance.

71

was shown in the high-styled but low-priced Chevrolets, the all-new Model A Fords, the sleeker Plymouths plus a broad range of medium-priced automobiles offered by dozens of manufacturers.

Financial collapse, fueled by the stock market crash in the fall of 1929, created havoc in the industry with some companies forced into bankruptcy and most recording heavy losses. Franklin D. Roosevelt took office in March 1933, and Congress soon carried out his campaign pledge to rid the nation of prohibition. Millions of Americans were out of work, and bread lines formed in every major city. Automobile prices, along with those for everything else, tumbled. With total production in the automobile industry in 1932 the lowest for any year since 1918, plants were closed and dealerships by the hundreds went out of business.

But the American people did not lose their zest for motorcars. While many no longer could afford a new car, new or used, they still found excitement in just looking at the handsome L-29 Cord, the awesome Duesenberg, the striking Packards, the new Franklins, the classic Lincolns, the beautiful Reo Royale, the sporty Hupmobiles and Buicks, the sleek new Stude-

bakers and Hudsons and the whole range of lower-priced models, all of which reflected a new concept known as styling. "Design" from the beginning of the auto industry originated in and was the province of the engineering department, but "styling" was the handiwork of artists and other creative minds. It started with Harley Earle at General Motors, who lent grace and form to the LaSalle, introduced in 1927 as a companion to the Cadillac.

Not all companies were equipped from either a financial or a personnel standpoint to apply the styling mystique to their new models, now declared to be essential to survival. So they turned to skilled coachbuilders and custom-body designers. Such names as LeBaron, Dietrich, Murphy, Brunn, Darrin, Brewster, Rollston, Judkins, Willoughby, Holbrook and Locke lent distinction to the offerings of numerous car manufacturers.

Because many of their innovative creations were built virtually by hand, production of custom-bodied cars was limited and prices were high. This added a new sense of exclusiveness to the ownership of one of these classic automobiles. They had a special appeal, as a result, to celebrities in all walks of life.

Not many Packard employees could afford to buy the cars they helped build, as evidenced by this photograph of one of the company's parking lots in Detroit, taken on a typical overcast day in Detroit during the pit of the Depression in 1932.

DETROIT PUBLIC LIBRARY

The success of an automobile dealer depended largely on how successful he was in selling the used cars he took in trade for new models. The Hupmobile factory in Detroit released this picture, taken in Detroit in the winter of 1931, to illustrate the importance of displaying a daily special.

Alvan T. Fuller, longtime Packard distributor in the New England area, shown earlier with his family and a 1905 Packard, was governor of Massachusetts when this picture was taken. The car is a splendid 1926 Packard Second Series Eight sedan-cabriolet with a custom Holbrook body.

Frankie Frisch, the great switch-hitting second baseman, was photographed in the snow with his 1926 Packard Six phaeton soon after he learned he had been traded by the New York Giants to the St. Louis Cardinals. Frisch was one of the author's sports idols back then, along with such other scrappy Cardinals as Chick Hafey and Sunny Jim Bottomley. Frisch had a lifetime batting average of .316 and served as manager of St. Louis, Pittsburgh and Chicago teams in the National League. He was named to the National Baseball Hall of Fame in 1947.

An air of serene dignity is apparent in this photograph of Queen Marie of Roumania, entering her 1926 Packard seven-passenger touring car which is about to lead a parade.

At the time this picture of Pauline Starke with a 1926 Packard Eight runabout was taken, the MGM star was filming the classic **An American Tragedy.** *She already had appeared in 112 movies.*

Soon after becoming U.S. women's amateur golf champion in 1926, Mrs. G. Stetson was photographed with this 1926 Packard Six phaeton.

Here is Louise Fazenda again, this time on the running board of a 1926 Cadillac roadster. The talented comedienne was as successful in silent pictures as she was in talkies. Among her best films were **The Beautiful and the Damned** *in 1922,* **Cuban Love Song** *in 1931 and* **The Casino Murder Case** *in 1935. Born in Lafayette, Indiana in 1895, she died in 1962.*

With her hand on the fender of her 1926 Lincoln sedan is film actress Vilma Banky. Born in Hungary in 1898 as Vilma Lonchit, she was discovered in Europe by Samuel Goldwyn. In Hollywood she began a meteoric rise as a silent screen star in 1925. She played opposite Rudolph Valentino, Gary Cooper and Ronald Colman. When this photo was taken, she was filming **The Son of the Shiek,** with Valentino. She retired with the coming of sound pictures.

Standing by his 1926 Packard Eight touring car is General William L. Mitchell, staunch advocate of air power during a time when most American military leaders believed in building naval strength and infantry forces. He commanded U.S. air forces in France in World War I and was promoted to brigadier general. After the armistice Billy Mitchell, as he was known by his supporters, was made director of military aviation. He argued volubly for a large, independent air force. Demoted and court-martialed in 1926, about the time this photo was taken, he continued until his death ten years later to be a bitter critic of army and government policy.

Attired in his custom-tailored knickers is golfer Walter Hagen, standing on the running board of his 1926 Cadillac brougham. Hagen won the PGA title five times and the British Open on four occasions.

In a posed publicity picture, Notre Dame University's fabled Knute Rockne instructs his varsity linemen, in front of a 1926 Studebaker Standard Six club coupe that was presented to him by admiring alumni. Rockne was born in Voss, Norway in 1888. He was named Notre Dame coach in 1914 and served until his death on March 31, 1931, in the crash of a Trans-Continental & Western Airways airplane near Bazaar, Kansas.

A pair of New York socialites meet on the road. Behind the wheel of the 1926 Packard Eight runabout is Mrs. Frederick Cameron Church, Jr. (a Vanderbilt), and astride the horse is Godfrey Bonnell. The original photo was taken by Pictorial Press Photos, New York.

Hal Roach Studios in 1926 used a fleet of Chevrolets on film location from its headquarters on the Big Horn Ranch near Moapa, Nevada.

Standing by his 1926 Packard Eight sedan is Frank B. Kellogg, internationally recognized diplomat and peacemaker. He served as U.S. senator from Minnesota from 1917 to 1923, and subsequently served as ambassador to Great Britain. After succeeding Charles Evans Hughes as secretary of state, he worked to better relations with Mexico and in 1928 promoted the Kellogg-Briand Pact, for which he was awarded the Nobel Peace Prize a year later.

While his exploits have not left a deep mark in the annals of automotive history, Willard "Big Boy" Rader, pictured behind the wheel of this 1927 LaSalle roadster, had the distinction of driving the pace cars in three Indianapolis 500 races. He piloted a LaSalle in the 1927 event, a Cadillac V-12 in the 1931 race and a LaSalle again in 1934. A Cadillac engineer, Rader is probably best known for having driven a 1927 LaSalle roadster at the General Motors proving ground 951.9 miles, with only nine stops for fuel and tire inspection, and averaging 95.3 miles per hour in less than ten hours behind the wheel. The attractive LaSalle was introduced in 1927 as a companion to the Cadillac. It was produced through the 1940 model year.

If one Hollywood actress can be said to have been a symbol of the flapper era, it has to be Clara Bow, shown here in her new 1927 LaSalle roadster. Her career spanned eleven years, from 1923 to 1933, starting with the film, **Down to the Sea in Ships,** but her most famous picture was **It** made in 1927, from a story and script by Elinor Glyn. Thereafter she was known as America's "It Girl."

Another Hollywood actress who liked the new 1927 LaSalle roadster was Laura LaPlante. Born in St. Louis in 1904, she was by the early 1920s Universal's top feminine star. She played in several Hoot Gibson movies, but is best remembered as the heroine of the spooky melodrama **The Cat and the Canary** in 1927.

The passenger in this 1927 Packard Eight runabout is Mary Katherine Campbell, who had the distinction of reigning as Miss America for two consecutive years (1922 and 1923). Behind the wheel is Bernice Rogers, junior prom queen of Ohio State University in 1927.

Richard Tauber, one of the world's great tenors, is pictured with his stylish six-cylinder Mercedes which he ordered in Vienna on February 19, 1927 and which was delivered to him in Berlin in April of that year. Note the inscription "Tauber Special" on the grille. Born in Linz, Austria, he achieved considerable renown in German, Italian and French repertories, but particularly in Mozart's operas. In 1924 he became a friend of Franz Lehár, who persuaded him to turn from opera to operetta. He wrote a succession of operettas which starred Tauber and made him honored throughout Europe. Tauber sang "Dein Ist Mein Ganzes Herz" ("Yours Is My Heart Alone") more than 15,000 times.

One of America's greatest sports writers and columnists, Grantland Rice, was photographed on a New York street with his 1927 Packard sedan. The picture was taken by John Adams Davis.

Germany's President Paul von Hindenburg received this Mercedes-Benz as a present on his eightieth birthday in 1927. The photograph probably was taken in the "Tiergarten," a large park in the center of Berlin.

He was a long way from New York's Yankee Stadium when Babe Ruth, the immortal baseball slugger, was photographed with this 1927 Moon Six-Sixty cabriolet roadster. He was in Vancouver, British Columbia on a vaudeville engagement after the 1926 baseball season ended. Perhaps the St. Louis-built car's model number had something to do with the fact that in the following year Ruth hit sixty home runs, a seasonal record that would stand until 1961 when Roger Maris, another Yankee, hammered out sixty-one.

Appearing again is glamorous Hollywood actress Pauline Starke who waits for her elegant chauffeur-driven 1927 Packard Third Series Eight town car with its custom body. She appeared in three films in 1927 — **The Perfect Sap, Captain Salvation** *and* **Dance Magic.**

William Randolph Hearst, Jr., son of the founder of the Hearst empire, is shown with Miss Dorothy Shea of Portland, Oregon, in a 1927 Packard Eight roadster. He began his newspaper career with the **New York American** *in 1928, as a reporter.*

With his 1927 Studebaker President sedan is John Erskine, American novelist, poet and essayist. He also served as president and director of the Juilliard Musical Foundation and director of the Metropolitan Opera Association. When this photograph was taken, he was a professor at Columbia University. Among his popular novels were **The Private Life of Helen of Troy** *and* **Sir Galahad.**

Ben Selvin and his dance orchestra played at the fashionable Cafe de Paris in New York in the 1920s. Here he poses with his violin on the running board of his 1927 Packard club sedan. The photograph was taken by Nick Lazarnick.

John N. Willys (with cane) founded the Toledo-based Willys-Overland Company which in more than a half century sold millions of Overland, Willys-Knight and Whippet cars. He is shaking hands with E. G. "Cannon Ball" Baker, noted auto test driver. Baker drove this low-priced Whippet coast to coast, achieving better than thirty miles per gallon of gasoline. During a long career, he set numerous endurance and speed records with many different automobiles — including Franklin, Revere, Stutz, Rickenbacker, Nash and Kaiser-Frazer.

One of the slickest second basemen who ever played professional baseball and a member of baseball's Hall of Fame, Charlie Gehringer of the Detroit Tigers, steps into his new 1927 Oakland Six landau coupe. He bought the car from G. A. Richards, Pontiac-Oakland distributor in Detroit, who also was a longtime owner of radio station WJR in the Motor City as well as of WGAR in Cleveland.

Charles M. Schwab, the American steel magnate, is in the front seat of this 1927 Packard Eight dual-cowl phaeton, photographed on an MGM set in Hollywood. Mrs. Schwab is in the back. Schwab worked his way up to the presidency of Carnegie Steel Company in 1897 and served as first president of U.S. Steel from 1901 to 1903. He resigned to head Bethlehem Steel Company, which he built into the largest independent steel empire in the world.

Alfred P. Sloan, Jr., president of General Motors, is pictured with a 1927 Series AA Chevrolet coach. The neat little car looks spotless, but why is there no tire on the spare rim?

*Photographed on a Hollywood studio lot with a beautiful 1927 Cadillac sport phaeton is actor Ralph Forbes. Note the dual cowl, visible just behind his right shoulder. Forbes appeared in fifty-four movies from 1926 to 1944, including such classics as **Beau Geste** in 1926, **Smilin' Through** in 1932, **Barretts of Wimpole Street** in 1934, **Mary of Scotland** in 1936 and **Kidnapped** in 1938.*

*Pictured with another 1927 Cadillac sport phaeton, wearing a sailor straw hat, is Will Rogers. As one biographer observed, Rogers was "an immensely popular entertainer and homespun philosopher, roving ambassador of rural Americana and spokesman of common folk everywhere." He starred with the Ziegfeld Follies on Broadway in 1917 before moving to Hollywood where he was an immediate box-office champion. Among his memorable motion pictures were **A Connecticut Yankee** in 1931, **State Fair** in 1933 and **David Harum** and **Judge Priest** in 1934. He died in an airplane crash with Wiley Post in 1935.*

When comedian Jimmy Durante was photographed with this 1927 Studebaker Dictator sedan, he was renowned for his antics on the stage. He did not make his first movie until 1930, **Roadhouse Nights.** *He went on to even greater heights on radio and television.*

On October 14, 1927, this Nash Ambassador sedan was presented to Prince William of Sweden (at wheel) by the Scandinavian employees of Nash Motors Company in Kenosha, Wisconsin. The royal crest of a gold crown and the letter W is on the door panel. Talking to the Prince is Mary Kerwin, a Nash employee.

During his 1927 visit to the United States, Prince William of Sweden was the guest of A. R. Erskine (right), president of Studebaker Corporation, in South Bend, Indiana. He was given use of a Studebaker President during his stay.

Count Felix von Luckner, the "Sea Devil" of the German Navy in World War I, stands beside a 1927 Studebaker President. During the war he commanded the **Seeadler,** a sailing ship equipped with hidden armament. Posing as a neutral cargo ship, its crew disguised in civilian clothes, the vessel would sail up to Allied ships carrying war materiel. Count von Luckner sank fourteen ships, including modern steamers, and took their crews prisoner. After the war, he toured the world and was acclaimed a hero by Germans and former foes alike. He was even decorated by the Pope as a "great humanitarian" for saving lives during his sea warfare and his courteous treatment of prisoners.

Soon after this photograph was taken in 1928, Charles Evans Hughes (center), was chosen chairman of the Pan-American Conference in Havana, Cuba. He was driven to the conference site in a 1927 Packard Six sedan. Hughes was appointed to the U.S. Supreme Court in 1910 by President Taft. He resigned in 1916 to run on the Republican ticket for president, narrowly losing to Woodrow Wilson. Presidents Harding and Coolidge named him secretary of state, and in 1930 President Hoover appointed him chief justice of the Supreme Court, a position he held until 1941.

Doris Eaton, a Hollywood bit player, posed with the snappy 1927 Chandler roadster in the Los Angeles area. A popular medium-priced car, the Chandler was made in Cleveland from 1913 to 1929.

One of Philadelphia's most prominent industrialists and philanthropists, A. Atwater Kent, sits behind the wheel of his 1927 Packard Eight phaeton. Kent began the manufacture of radio receiving sets in 1922 and was one of the first to sponsor radio programs, both at the national and the local levels. He restored the Betsy Ross home in Philadelphia in 1937 and also the Franklin Institute building which he acquired, restored and presented to the city of Philadelphia as a museum. The city in appreciation named it the Atwater Kent Museum.

BABY WAMPAS STARS — Inveterate moviegoers of the 1920's and early 1930's could tell you not only what a Baby Wampas star was but could probably name a few. But today ask anyone younger than sixty, and all you will get will be blank stares, or some wiseacre may guess they had something to do with Argentine grass. Wampas stood for Western Association of Motion Picture Advertisers, whose members each year from 1922 to 1934 voted to select the thirteen young starlets whom they deemed most likely to succeed. Some did, but many others never made it. In the beginning as much public interest was aroused by the selections as is demonstrated today by the Oscar awards.

In some years the winners reflected uncanny foresight on the part of the selectors. Clara Bow, for example, was a Wampas star of 1924 — and ponder this group for 1926 who made it: Mary Astor, Joan Crawford, Dolores Del Rio, Janet Gaynor and Fay Wray. Jean Arthur and Loretta Young were named in 1929, while Ginger Rogers was selected in 1932. Most of the Wampas stars of 1927 and 1928 are pictured here.

Shown with a 1927 Packard phaeton are (not necessarily in order as pictured): Patricia Avery, Rita Carewe, Helene Costello, Barbara Kent, Natalie Kingston, Gwen Lee, Mary McAlister, Gladys McConnell, Sally Phipps, Sally Rand, Martha Sleeper, Tris Stuart and Adamae Vaughn. Twelve of the thirteen girls chosen appear in the photograph.

Seven of the 1928 Wampas stars adorn the 1928 Cadillac sedan below. Molly O'Day is at the wheel while Lina Basquette is at far left next to Sue Carol. Gwen Lee (selected also in 1927) and Sally Eilers are sitting on the roof. Others in the picture could not be positively identified. The other 1928 Wampas stars were Flora Bramley, Ann Christy, June Collyer, Alice Day, Audrey Ferris, Dorothy Gulliver, Ruth Taylor and Lupe Velez.

A week after·this picture of Dolores Del Rio with her 1928 Cadillac seven-passenger sedan was taken, her new film **Ramona** opened in major theaters across the country. The Mexican-born actress was a major film star in both the United States and Mexico. The trophy in the picture was given to her as "the most popular Wampas Baby Star of 1928" by Don Lee, the Cadillac distributor for Southern California.

The lovable comedian Leon Erroll helps a lady from a 1928 Cadillac dual-cowl phaeton. Erroll was born in 1881 in Sydney, Australia. After starring on Broadway, beginning with the Ziegfeld Follies of 1911, until the mid-1920s, he went to Hollywood where he appeared in many movies, commencing with **Yolanda** in 1924. He made films until 1951, the year of his death. His last was **Footlight Varieties,** for RKO.

Clara Bow, the Hollywood siren, moved from a LaSalle to a Cadillac sedan in 1928. One writer referred to her as a "vibrant, liberated young woman of personal magnetism and boundless energy whose bobbed hair, cupid bow lips and sparkling eyes came to represent an era." She was born in 1906 and died in 1965.

Paramount actress Sally Blane was filming **Fools for Luck** when this 1928 Oakland landau sedan was introduced. She is pointing to the car's new radiator mascot exemplifying an American eagle in flight. Sally was born Elizabeth Jane Young in Salida, Colorado. One of her sisters is actress Loretta Young.

A 1928 Packard Eight stands ready to take Spain's King Alfonso XIII from the railroad station to the palace.

Milton C. Work, a prominent bridge-playing expert of the 1920s, bought this 1928 Packard Eight sedan from Packard's California distributor, Earle C. Anthony. Mr and Mrs. Work pose proudly with the new car.

Perhaps no one in the history of motion pictures could scream more dramatically than Fay Wray, the Canadian-born actress who soared to fame in Erich von Stroheim's **The Wedding March** in 1928, but who is best remembered for her role in **King Kong** in 1933 as the damsel in distress. She is not screaming but smiling here, with her 1928 Packard Six Model 526 convertible coupe.

Douglas Fairbanks and Mary Pickford were friends of Mr. and Mrs. Edsel Ford, so when the long-awaited all-new Model A Ford came out in 1928, they were among the first to get one. Mary Pickford was married three times — first to Owen Moore, then to Fairbanks. After Fairbanks died, she married Charles "Buddy" Rogers.

Harry Lauder, the noted Scottish entertainer, appears again, explaining to onlookers that the new 1928 Ford Model A is a completely different car from the famed Model T it replaced. Lauder's real name was Harry MacLennan. He died at eighty in 1950.

*One film biographer called Dolores Del Rio, shown stepping out of a 1928 Ford sport coupe, "one of the most beautiful women ever to grace the American screen." She was a star from her first picture, **What Price Glory?** in 1927. Two of her finest films were **Maria Candelaria,** directed in 1943 by Emilio Fernandez, and **The Fugitive,** directed in 1947 by John Ford.*

*The 1928 Model A Ford was one of Cecil B. DeMille's alltime favorite cars. The Hollywood producer had owned three Locomobiles, one of which he drove for fourteen years, a Cunningham and a Lincoln when he purchased this tudor sedan. Later he owned a 1937 Cord 810. DeMille (1881-1959) made his acting debut on Broadway in 1900. He went into partnership in 1913 with vaudeville musician Jesse L. Laskey and glove salesman Samuel Goldfish (later Goldwyn). They formed a motion picture firm and traveled to Hollywood to produce their first film, **The Squaw Man,** in 1914. A colossal picture six reels in length, it was a critical success. The Laskey company grew into Paramount Pictures. A born showman, DeMille produced and directed seventy pictures, including **King of Kings** in 1927 and **The Ten Commandments** in 1956. From 1936 to 1945 he hosted the popular Lux Radio Theatre on network radio.*

At the wheel of a 1928 Chrysler Seventy-Five roadster is the remarkable Amelia Earhart, who from the time of her first airplane ride in Glendale, California in 1919 until her still-unsolved disappearance in an around-the-world flight with Frederick Noonan in 1937, was the world's foremost aviatrix. On June 17, 1928, with pilot Wilmer Stultz and mechanic Lou Gordon, she flew in a Fokker trimotor across the Atlantic from Newfoundland to Wales. The hop took only twenty hours and forty minutes.

Photographed in Philadelphia's Shibe Park with his new 1928 Packard Six sedan is Eddie Rommel, star pitcher for the Philadelphia Athletics in the American League.

Photographed on a New York street with his unusual 1928 Packard Eight convertible sedan is the entertainer Al Jolson. The custom-built car does not incorporate the famous Packard radiator design. Born in 1886 as Asa Yoelson, Al Jolson was a major Broadway attraction before starring in the first talking picture, **The Jazz Singer,** in 1927.

Rene Lacoste, tennis star of the 1920 s, is at the wheel of this 1928 Packard Eight touring, photographed at the entrance to the Packard Motor Car Company offices in Detroit. Lacoste was U.S. Tennis Association men's singles national champion in 1926 and 1927.

*Public recognition of the talents of Norman Rockwell, shown here with his 1928 Packard Six sedan, continues to grow. Best known for his magazine covers, notably for the **Saturday Evening Post,** Rockwell was a gifted artist and illustrator. He loved to depict, with great clarity and detail, scenes from daily small-town life. His Four Freedoms murals, in the Nassau Tavern at Princeton, New Jersey, are American classics. The photograph was taken by John Adams Davis.*

Pictured with a 1928 Franklin sport runabout is Hollywood actor Edmund Lowe. The star of many films, he is remembered perhaps more for his role as the roughneck Sergeant Quirt in the silent version of **What Price Glory?** *than for any other. The Franklin car was made in Syracuse, New York from 1901 to 1934.*

The popular Franklin car was powered by an air-cooled engine, the same type as used in airplanes, so it was only natural that after Charles A. Lindbergh's solo flight across the Atlantic, the Franklin company would give him a car. This rather dark photograph of Lindbergh with his new sedan was taken in a hangar next to the Ryan monoplane "Spirit of St. Louis" that took him on the famous flight. Several years later Lindbergh gave the car to the Henry Ford Museum in Dearborn, Michigan.

Actor James Dunn poses with his 1928 Franklin town car which has a custom body by Holbrook. The theater marquee in the background indicates he was appearing in person. The photograph was taken in New York City before Dunn's debut in Hollywood because his first film, **Bad Girl,** *was not made until 1931. He won the Academy Award for best supporting actor in 1945 for* **A Tree Grows in Brooklyn.**

Waving from a 1928 Auburn speedster is Roscoe Ates, the Hollywood comic actor who played in many important films including **Billy the Kid** *in 1930,* **The Champ** *in 1931 and* **Gone With The Wind** *in 1939. Auburn cars, always noted for their advanced design, were built in Auburn, Indiana from 1900 to 1935.*

Shown with his 1928 Packard Eight club sedan is Fielding H. Yost, coach of the University of Michigan's famed "point-a-minute" football teams from 1901 to 1927. His teams won 164, lost twenty-nine and tied ten. Yost was named athletic director at Michigan in 1921.

The front-seat passenger in this classic 1928 Mercedes-Benz sports car is the Japanese motion picture star Nagamasa Kawakita, from Tokyo. The photograph was taken at the northern entrace to the Avus, a straight race track leading ten km. toward Potsdam, in East Germany.

Pioneer race driver Ralph dePalma is behind the wheel of his Mercedes-Benz sports model S in which he won two races at the Atlantic City race track on May 30, 1928.

Roger W. Babson, internationally known statistician and economist and founder of Babson Institute, prepares to enter his 1928 Packard Six sedan. Born in Gloucester, Massachusetts in 1875, he was the Prohibition Party candidate for president of the United States in 1940. He died in 1967.

98

The handsomely-attired owner standing beside his 1928 Packard Eight seven-passenger touring is Charles "Buddy" Rogers, the popular Paramount film star, who wants us also to meet Baron, his "police dog," as a German shepherd frequently was called then. The car is finished in black, with a red line around the body. Rogers, who became Mary Pickford's third husband in 1936, made four films in 1929 — **Close Harmony, Illusion, River of Romance** *and* **Half-Way to Heaven.**

Pictured with a 1928 Pontiac roadster are Paramount film players Nora Lane and Chester Conklin, both of whom appeared in **Jesse James** *in 1927. It was Miss Lane's first picture. Conklin was a pioneer movie comedian in the slapstick era of two-reel silents. He appeared in hundreds of Mack Sennett shorts, often making two Keystone Kops pictures in a week. His last full-length film was* **Beautiful Blonde from Bashful Bend** *in 1949. The Pontiac made its bow in 1926, produced at that time by the Oakland Motor Car Company, a division of General Motors.*

Posing leisurely with a 1928 Pontiac sedan is the motion picture actor Richard Dix. Born in St. Paul, Minnesota as Ernest Carlton Brimmer, he made his Hollywood debut in 1921 in **Dangerous Curve Ahead.** Among his notable silent film roles was as an Indian in **The Vanishing American** in 1925. One of his best-known early sound pictures was **Cimarron** in 1931.

Billy Sunday, the famous American evangelist, bought a 1928 Studebaker President Eight sedan. Before becoming an evangelist in 1896, he had been a professional baseball player, from 1883 to 1890. He was born in Ames, Iowa in 1863 and died in 1935.

Gwen Lee, Metro-Goldwyn-Mayer featured player shown with her 1928 Packard Eight runabout, had a very busy year in 1928, appearing in five films, **Making Sharp Shooters, Her Wild Oat, Laugh, Clown, Laugh, The Actress** and **Show Girl.**

Samuel Lionel Rothafel, better known as Roxy, is behind the wheel of his custom-built Cunningham roadster, as his chauffeur looks on. Minnesota-born Roxy was a famous theatrical producer and impresario who was managing director of many New York theaters and founded the Rockettes, the widely acclaimed singing and dancing group. New York's Roxy Theater was built especially for him in 1927. After it opened, he was paid $2,000 a week plus ten per cent of the profits to manage it. He also was a pioneer in radio broadcasting, hosting a folksy variety show called "Roxy and His Gang."

Aviation pioneer Eddie Stinson poses proudly with his 1928 Essex coach, produced by Hudson Motor Car Company. An early test pilot, he formed Stinson Aircraft Corporation in Detroit to build the celebrated Stinson-Detroiter. He also built the Stinson Junior, a four-place cabin model. In 1932 while piloting a Junior from Chicago to Detroit, he tried to make an emergency landing in a small park but clipped a flagpole and died later in a hospital.

AN ANHEUSER-BUSCH AUTOMOBILE?

One of the most resourceful private enterprises in America for nearly thirteen decades has been Anheuser-Busch of St. Louis. Throughout the world today its famous Budweiser beer commands wide acceptance and respect. Yet there was a time when the company's sole dependence on the brewing and marketing of beer almost led to its failure.

It was during prohibition — from World War I until 1933. But Anheuser-Busch's management took vigorous action as early as 1916 to forestall financial disaster. The company began to promote and sell its brewers' yeast around the world, strengthened its sales abroad (production of beer for export was not banned) and it introduced a distinctive new beverage with a negligible alcoholic content that *tasted* like beer. Called Bevo, it was made from barley malt, rice, hops, yeast and water. It derived its name from the Bohemian word "pivo," meaning beer. Produced by a hastened fermentation, it was an instant success when it was first marketed in 1916. Bevo soon was being sold all over the world, with five million cases shipped in 1918.

Bevo was so popular, in fact, that Anheuser-Busch's vehicle department built a special motorized vehicle called the "Bevo Boat" which it offered to the United States Government for use in promoting sales of war bonds. The unusual vehicle, mounted on a Pierce-Arrow chassis, looked more like a boat than an automobile, but it drew attention and sold bonds (and Bevo) wherever it went.

This same vehicle department during prohibition designed and manufactured hundreds of truck and bus bodies which Anheuser-Busch sold in significant numbers. It made A.B.C. refrigerator truck bodies, armored car bodies for banks, and other bodies for general utility and heavy hauling. It developed the "Lampsteed Kampkar" containing built-in beds and cooking equipment for campers, on a Ford Model T chassis, and a model called "The Rancher" that resembled modern station wagons, on Dodge, Chevrolet and Ford chassis. It also produced large bus bodies for passenger lines and schools, as well as a popular horse van.

Meanwhile, Americans were having fun breaking the law. By the millions they frequented illegal saloons called speakeasies, bought illicit hard liquor from bootleggers and even found ways to make their own alcoholic beverages. And when Congress relented a bit and legalized the making of beer at home, "home brew" took the country by storm. Many householders bought yeast made by Anheuser-Busch, but the trend hastened the decline in the sale of Bevo, which by 1929 was discontinued altogether.

The Bevo Boat, however, still drew crowds wherever it went. Anheuser-Busch built three other versions of the vehicle which with the impending demise of Bevo became known as "the Budweiser car."

The first Bevo Boat traveled the country promoting the sale of war bonds, beginning in 1917. Obviously 1917 vehicles did not have tires or wheels like those shown, but in this retouched photograph the body is the same as was on the original vehicle.

The second model was larger and resembled a boat even more than the first.

ANHEUSER-BUSCH COMPANIES

This photograph, taken in 1925, shows the third version — replete with bell, new snout-like front end and other garish touches.

The Bevo Boat made its appearance at the Indianapolis Motor Speedway for the 1929 500-mile race. That's Barney Oldfield, the pioneer race driver, in the front passenger seat.

Standing beside his 1929 Cadillac Fleetwood transformable cabriolet in New York's Central Park is the debonair mayor of America's largest city, James J. Walker. During his time in office, from 1925 to 1932, he backed adoption of an extensive transit system, unified the public hospitals and created the department of sanitation. Frauds, however, were exposed in the municipal government and the state legislature ordered an investigation. Fifteen charges were leveled at Walker, who resigned in 1932. He lived in Europe for a number of years before his death at sixty-five, in 1946.

While this classic Duesenberg bears a 1935 California license plate, the car is a 1929 dual-cowl phaeton, custom-built by Murphy. Five unidentified starlets are posing in this photograph, taken on a Hollywood studio lot. S. R. Nicholson, an eminent automotive historian, calls the Model J Duesenberg "the most remarkable automobile in America — bigger, faster, more elaborate and more expensive than any other." Duesenberg made only the chassis, costing $8,500, with the body custom-built. The last Duesenbergs were produced in 1937.

With her new 1929 Buick Country Club convertible coupe is Gertrude Ederle, who not only was the first woman to swim the English Channel, but the first to do it using a crawl stroke. The native-born New Yorker made the crossing in fourteen hours and thirty-one minutes on August 6, 1926.

Ruth Elder, who played the leading role opposite Richard Dix in Paramount's **Moran of the Marines,** posed with a new 1929 Buick close-coupled five-passenger sedan "while awaiting the call to action in her first motion picture," according to the caption for this Paramount publicity picture. It was her only film.

Looking at a front-wheel-drive 1929 Ruxton sedan with a U.S. naval officer is Hans von Schiller (right), commander of the German dirigible **Graf Zeppelin** *which had just completed a trip with passengers across the Atlantic. The ill-fated Ruxton, famous for its low silhouette and unusual exterior paint schemes, was built briefly in various automobile plants, primarily in St. Louis, with fewer than 700 produced altogether.*

Film actress Anita Page reached her peak in 1929, when this LaSalle sedan was built, with **The Broadway Melody.** *She was born Anita Pomares, of Spanish descent, in Flushing, New York in 1910. This photograph was taken on the MGM lot in Culver City, California.*

Two Hollywood greats pose with a 1929 Chevrolet convertible landau — Harold Lloyd, at the wheel, and Hal Roach, standing.

When this picture of Neil Hamilton with a 1929 Willys Eight coupe was taken, the Paramount actor was filming **The Mysterious Dr. Fu Manchu.** A native of Lynn, Massachusetts, Hamilton got his first big opportunity in D. W. Griffith's **The White Rose** in 1923. He became Paramount's most popular leading man of the 1920s and continued active in Hollywood until the 1970s. Many readers will remember him also as Police Commissioner Gordon in TV's "Batman" series of the early 1960s. Willys-Overland, one of the leading independent U.S. auto companies, built Willys, Willys-Knight and Whippet cars in 1929.

Wearing a firm look of determination, the Sultan of Koeta Pinang in the Dutch East Indies enters his 1929 Packard Sixth Series Custom Eight touring car.

It was a cold, brisk day on March 4, 1929 when Herbert Hoover was inaugurated as president of the United States. He is riding in the official White House Pierce-Arrow touring car, seated next to the retiring president, Calvin Coolidge.

MVMA

106

The great "march king," John Philip Sousa, had the use of this 1929 Studebaker President Eight during his band's appearance at Convention Hall in Tulsa, Oklahoma in October 1928. Sousa, who was born in Washington, D.C. in 1854, played in Offenbach's orchestra at the Centennial Exhibition in Philadelphia in 1876, was named bandmaster for the U.S. Marine Corps in 1880 and formed the world-renowned Sousa's Band in 1892. He composed more than 100 stirring marches, including "The Washington Post," "Semper Fidelis" and "Stars and Stripes Forever."

For years after he lost the heavyweight boxing title to Gene Tunney, Jack Dempsey gathered crowds of admirers. Here he is entering his 1929 Chrysler Imperial Model L roadster.

Morton Downey, popular crooner on radio and in motion pictures, owned this 1929 Hudson sedan. He appeared in three films in 1929, including **Mother's Boy.**

The famous Italian tenor Tito Schipa, shown with his wife and daughter, owned this 1929 Nash Advanced Six coupe. He was engaged by the Chicago Civic Opera from 1920 to 1932. His first appearance with the Metropolitan was on November 23, 1932.

In the days of silent films, theater owners in major cities installed huge pipe organs and hired talented organists to play during the showing of the films. One of the best was Stanleigh Malotte, who played at the Olympia Theatre in Miami. He and Mrs. Malotte are shown with their new 1929 Packard Standard Eight coupe.

Hollywood actress Raquel Torres gets into her 1929 Packard Standard Eight Model 633 runabout. She had just finished the film, **The Bridge of San Luis Rey,** playing the role of Pepita. Born in Hermosillo, Mexico as Paula Osterman, she was a star after her first picture, **White Shadows of the South Seas** in 1928. However, after making only seven pictures, she retired to marry a wealthy businessman. Widowed, she married actor Jon Hall in 1959.

TONY MITCHELL COLLECTION

On a Hollywood set with her 1929 Stearns-Knight Deluxe Eight convertible coupe is stage and screen actress Lillian Roth. Her career reached its peak in the late 1920s and early 1930s when she starred on stage in "Earl Carroll's Vanities" and Ziegfeld's "Midnight Frolics." In 1953, on the television program "This Is Your Life," she told the tragic story of how her career was wrecked by alcoholism and eight divorces. In the following year her autobiography **I'll Cry Tomorrow** became an international best seller. The Stearns-Knight was built in Cleveland by F. B. Stearns Company which began producing automobiles in 1899.

109

His Highness, the Prince of Asturias and crown prince of Spain, is seated in the back (closest to camera) of this 1929 Packard DeLuxe Eight touring car. The picture was taken during a summer visit to the royal palace of the Magdalena at Santandar. A Lalique glass comet is mounted on the front fender.

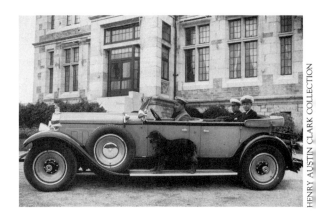

Prominent engineering alumni of Purdue University presented this 1929 Packard Model 640 sedan to the university's president, Edward C. Elliott.

Photographed on a Hollywood set is actress Doris Hill, in the front seat of a snappy 1929 Hupmobile Century Eight sportster. A leading lady of films from the late 1920s to early 1930s, she made three pictures in 1929, **Murder Mystery**, **His Glorious Night** and **Darkened Rooms**.

Irene Rich, star of many screen melodramas of the 1920s, poses grandly with her 1929 Packard all-weather town car as her chauffeur waits. Born Irene Luther in Buffalo in 1891, she had her first chance in films as an extra in Mary Pickford's **Stella Marris** *in 1918. With the advent of sound, she played maternal roles. She teamed with Will Rogers as his nagging wife in several pictures. Miss Rich retired from the screen in 1932 to become a popular radio star with the long-running program, "Dear John." She returned to Hollywood after six years, playing various character roles.*

Posing with a 1929 Oakland All-American six-cylinder convertible cabriolet is Doree Leslie, who appeared with Ed Wynn in the Broadway musical, **Manhattan Mary**.

Johnny Kuck, who took first place in the shot put at the 1928 Olympic Games in Amsterdam, is shown with his 1929 Oakland All-American six-cylinder sport roadster.

With her 1929 Oakland sedan is Mary Brian, Paramount star. She appeared in films originally as Wendy in **Peter Pan**, produced in 1924. From then until 1943, she starred in fifty-one more pictures, including **Beau Geste** in 1926, **The Virginian** in 1929 and **The Front Page** in 1931. In 1953 she played the mother in the TV series, "Meet Corliss Archer."

The Marx Brothers were on hand when the classic Cord L-29 front-drive cars were introduced in 1929. They are shown here with four convertible models in front of the English Opera House in Indianapolis. The Cord was the creation of Erret Lobban Cord, who at the time also was building the Duesenberg and the Auburn, all in Indiana. In vaudeville from childhood, the Marx Brothers came to Hollywood following brilliant success on Broadway. Three of their most memorable films were **Animal Crackers** in 1930, **Horse Feathers** in 1932 and the hilarious **A Night at the Opera** in 1935.

Film actor Richard Dix shows up again, this time backing out of his mother's driveway in a 1929 Pierce-Arrow with a custom Don Lee body. Five of the eighty-three pictures Dix made were released in 1929 — **The Wheel of Life, Nothing but the Truth, Seven Keys to Baldplate, Redskin** and **The Love Doctor.**

Internationally renowned champion figure skater Sonja Henie smiles from her 1929 Packard Eight roadster. Born in Oslo, Norway in 1912, she won her first world figure skating championship in 1927. She went on to capture gold medals in three Olympiads and to star in Hollywood films and in her own Hollywood Ice Revues. She became a U.S. citizen in 1941.

*Actress Lenore Ulrich poses with her 1929 LaSalle sport phaeton. In 1915 she became a protege of stage producer David Belasco, who made her into an important Broadway star. While appearing on the stage, she occasionally starred in silent and early sound films. She appeared in **Camille** with Greta Garbo, in 1937.*

When President-elect Franklin D. Roosevelt toured western Pennsylvania shortly after his election in November 1932, automobiles for him and his party were furnished by the Packard distributor in Pittsburgh. The open car in which he is riding is a 1929 DeLuxe Eight touring, presumably the most appropriate model available.

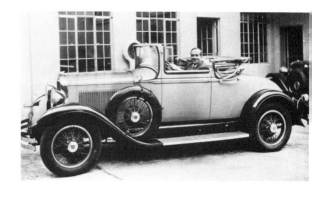

One motion picture historian described Al Jolson, shown here with a 1929 Studebaker Commander cabriolet, as a great entertainer "with an inimitable voice and electric presence." He was a star on television in its early days, as well as in many motion pictures.

It's Al Jolson again, this time with a custom-built 1929 Mercedes and his wife, actress Ruby Keeler.

Talented actress Lupe Velez stands beside her 1929 Marmon 78 sedan. She made her first picture, **The Gaucho,** in 1927, and twenty-eight more after that, but who can forget her moving performance with Lawrence Tibbett in **Cuban Love Song,** in 1931? Lupe Velez, born Guadaloupe Velez deVillabos, began her career as a dancer in Mexico City at thirteen. Florenz Ziegfeld brought her to New York in 1932 to play Conchita in **Hot-Cha.** She was married in 1933 to John Weissmuller, Olympic swimmer and star of the Tarzan series.

E. G. "Cannon Ball" Baker (second from left) is pictured with the 1929 Franklin, powered with the new 1930-type engine, with which he established a new transcontinental record of sixty-nine hours 31 minutes in 1929. To his right is Hugh Goodhart, Franklin advertising manager.

Recognized at the time as the oldest man in the world, Zaro Aha, of Turkey, posed with a 1929 air-cooled Franklin touring car. He claimed he was 156 years old.

Craig Wood, the professional golf champion from New Jersey, is pictured with the 1929 Studebaker President Eight roadster he bought from the Studebaker dealer in East Orange. Wood came in second in many thrilling golf tournaments and won the U.S. Open in Fort Worth in 1941. In the same year he barely bested Byron Nelson in winning the Masters at Augusta, Georgia.

Captain Charles Kingsford-Smith, pilot from Australia, and his crew of the "Southern Cross," a three-engine Fokker, flew across the Pacific in three jumps in 1928 — the first to do so. The noted airman, who was later knighted, is shown with a 1929 Packard Standard Eight sedan during a visit to Honolulu. With him is S. A. Campbell, one of Hawaii's leading motor enthusiasts of the day.

The American Austin, a genuinely small car, showed great promise when it bowed in 1930, here publicized with Bruce Rogers, Paramount screen player. So accustomed to larger "standard-sized" automobiles were Americans that Austin copywriters felt compelled to stress the fact that, indeed, it was a car that would run. Its advertising stressed the Austin had a speed in excess of fifty miles per hour and that its four-cylinder engine gave forty miles per gallon of fuel.

Many Austins were sold in Hollywood. The first model delivered to a private owner went to Al Jolson. Slim Summerville had his own ideas about getting into the tiny car. He appeared in forty-eight movies from 1927 to 1946. The American Austin was built in Butler, Pennsylvania from 1930 to 1935, when it became the American Bantam which survived until 1941.

Richard Bonelli, baritone of the Chicago Civic Opera Company, traveled in his 1930 Pierce-Arrow Straight Eight roadster, filling radio and concert engagements.

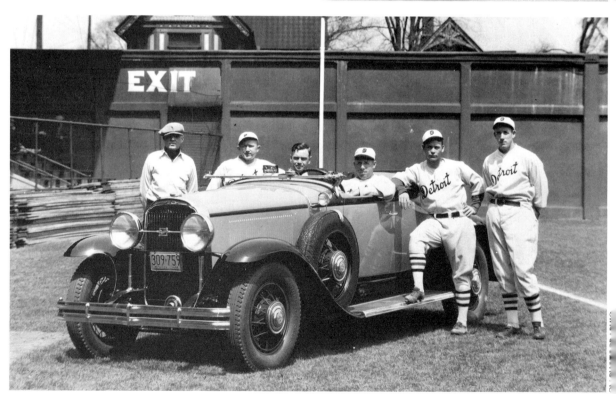

Left field in old Navin Field (now Tiger Stadium) was selected as the scene for this unusual picture of a group of Detroit Tigers with a 1930 Buick convertible coupe. From the left are groundskeeper Neil Conway, George Sucie, Owen Carroll, Bob Fothergill, Roy Johnson and Whitlow Wyatt. The author is indebted to Charlie Gehringer for making the identifications.

In a scene from one of many movies they made, perhaps the greatest comedy team of all time, Stan Laurel (left) and Oliver Hardy, wonder what is causing a traffic jam as they sit helplessly in their 1930 Buick. The hilarious antics of Laurel and Hardy, stars in both silent and talking pictures, continue to be appreciated by television audiences throughout the world who view their old films.

The automobile provided a perfect prop for Laurel and Hardy in many of their films. The Model T Ford especially helped appeal to their sense of the ridiculous.

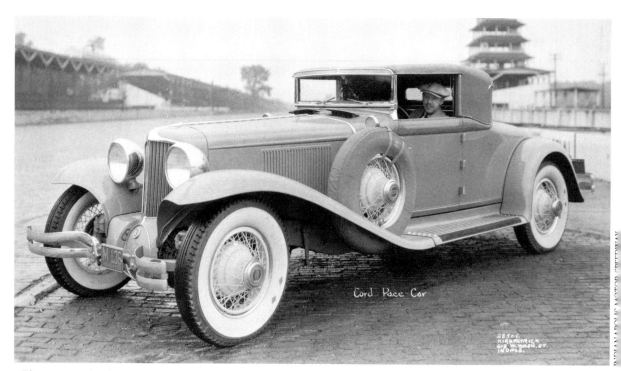

The pace car for the 1930 Indianapolis 500 race was this beautiful Cord cabriolet. The driver was scheduled to be E. L. Cord (at the wheel in this photograph), founder and president of the company that built the front-drive automobile, but at the last moment Wade Morton substituted for him.

The incomparable James Cagney in an incomparable 1930 Cord cabriolet. Following success on Broadway, Cagney went to Hollywood in the year this car was built, to co-star with Joan Blondell in **Sinners' Holiday**. He played a ruthless prohibition gangster in **The Public Enemy** in 1931 and thereafter was cast in cocky, pugnacious parts. In 1942 he won an Academy Award as best actor in **Yankee Doodle Dandy**.

Paul Whiteman, the renowned orchestra leader, stands with his 1930 Cord L-29 in front of the Vogue tire dealership in Los Angeles. He seems to be laughing, perhaps because he does not believe whitewall tires with two rows of large black X marks ever will be popular.

Behind the wheel of his 1930 Cord is Ronald Colman, the suave British-born actor with the unforgettable resonant voice. His first film success was **The White Sister** with Lillian Gish, in 1923. From then on he developed into one of Hollywood's most popular romantic stars. A few of his greatest pictures were **Arrowsmith** in 1931, **A Tale of Two Cities** in 1935 and **Lost Horizon** in 1937.

The original caption for this publicity photograph released in 1930 indicated that "this swanky-looking motor car won the Grand Prix at Monte Carlo recently." The car is a front-drive Cord with custom body designed by Alexis Sakhnoffsky, then with the Hayes Body Company. With the car is Marion Dodge, of the **Simple Simon** cast, playing at the Ziegfeld Theatre in New York.

121

This Paramount still shows stars Gary Cooper and Sylvia Sidney in a scene from **City Streets,** released in 1931. The car is a 1930 Lincoln. Cooper, born in Helena, Montana in 1901, got his big break in 1926 when he was the second lead in **The Winning of Barbara Worth**, starring Ronald Colman and Vilma Banky. A box-office hit, it started him on his way to becoming an alltime Hollywood great. He won two Oscars for best actor, in 1942 for **Sergeant York** and in 1952 for **High Noon.** Sylvia Sidney played heroine roles in many films, including **Ladies of the Big House** in 1932, **You Only Live Once** in 1937 and **Les Miserables** in 1953.

Charles Mack, of Moran & Mack, the famous "Two Black Crows" vaudeville team that later went on network radio, gets into his 1930 Minerva town car. The Minerva, an excellent and beautiful luxury car built in Belgium from 1900 to 1939, often had a custom-built body. From 1910 on, all Minervas used the Knight sleeve-valve engine.

This excellent photograph of a 1930 Oakland Eight sport roadster is being driven by a young lady identified in the GM Photographic files only as "the Blossom Queen."

GM PHOTOGRAPHIC

Charles A. Lindbergh, American aviation hero, owned a second Franklin. He is pictured in his 1930 convertible speedster, with a special Dietrich body.

The original caption for this publicity photograph, released July 18, 1930 by Duesenberg, Inc., of Indianapolis, reported: "Rear Admiral Richard E. Byrd, conquerer of both the North and the South Poles, is given a tremendous welcome in Chicago. He is shown in the rear seat (white uniform) in the official Duesenberg car which he used while in Chicago. With him in the rear seat is Rear Admiral Walter S. Crosley (left), commandant of the Great Lakes Naval Station; Al Dunlap (center), president of the Chicago Press Club, and Walter D. Saltiel (front seat), who represented Mayor Thompson."

It was the last year for the striking Ruxton. Pictured is a rare 1930 town car with actress Claire Windsor, who appeared in twenty-five films in the 1920s. Her last was **Captain Lash** in 1929. If this were intended to be a publicity picture, either for the actress or for the car, one cannot help wondering why someone did not first clean the whitewall tires.

Two great Hollywood performers use a 1930 Lincoln to pantomime a scene from a motion picture. On the running board is Buster Keaton, the noted comedian of silent and talking pictures, while behind the wheel is Cliff Edwards, a man of many talents. In 1936 he replaced Rudy Vallee on Broadway as star of **George White's Scandals**, and in 1929 he introduced the song "Singin' in the Rain" in the film **The Hollywood Revue**. His was the voice of Jiminy Cricket in Disney's classic **Pinocchio** in 1940.

*Perched on the tire mount of this 1930 Hupmobile Eight town sedan is Helen Kane, the famed "boop-boop-a-doop" girl. Born in 1930 as Helen Schroeder, she began her career in vaudeville with the Marx Brothers and made her Broadway debut in 1927 with **A Night in Spain**. A year later she created a sensation with her squeaky, childlike "boop-boop-a-doop" rendition of the song "I Wanna Be Loved by You," in the musical **Good Boy**. Her popularity led to a film contract with Paramount for whom she made six movies in 1929 and 1930.*

*The United States Advertising Corporation, of Toledo, Ohio, which handled West Coast publicity for the Franklin car in the early 1930s, released this photograph of Rosita Moreno, Paramount star, with a 1930 Franklin Pirate touring car. At the time she was between her first two pictures, **Her Wedding Night** and **The Santa Fe Trail**, both 1930 releases. She starred in many Mexican-made films for a number of years.*

125

With another 1930 Hupmobile Eight town sedan are actors Jack Oakie (at wheel) and Harry Green, who appeared together in **Paramount on Parade** in 1930. Oakie, born Lewis Delaney Offield in 1903 in Sedalia, Missouri, played in scores of screen productions, in both leads and supporting roles. One of his most memorable was in Chaplin's **The Great Dictator** in 1940. Green appeared in twenty-five pictures from 1929 to 1960.

Margaret Culkin Banning, noted novelist, stands beside the 1930 Packard Standard Eight sedan she purchased from the Packard dealer in Duluth, Minnesota. Among her popular novels were **A Handmaid of the Lord**, published in 1924, **The Iron Will** in 1935, **Give Us Our Years** in 1949, **The Convert** in 1957 and **Mesabi** in 1969.

Standing in front of a 1930 Packard Custom Eight roadster are Hollywood stars Carole Lombard and Lyle Talbot. She was born Jane Alice Peters in Fort Wayne, Indiana in 1908. One of Hollywood's most talented and glamorous performers of the 1930s, she probably is best remembered for her role in **My Man Godfrey** in 1936. Miss Lombard married William Powell in 1931 and divorced him two years later. She was married to Clark Gable when she was killed in an airplane crash in 1942. Talbot, born Lisle Henderson in 1902 in Pittsburgh, played leading roles in B films and appeared on several prominent television shows, including "The Burns and Allen Show" and "Ozzie and Harriet."

*Actress Polly Walker had just finished filming **Hit the Deck** in 1930 when she was photographed with this Packard Eight sport phaeton in San Francisco. She came to Hollywood following her success in Broadway musicals, including Ziegfeld's **No Foolin'** in 1926.*

*This photograph of Hollywood actress Dorothy Jordan and a 1930 Packard Eight convertible coupe was taken by William Grimes of Metro Goldwyn & Mayer studios. She appeared in four films in 1930, including **Call of the Flesh** with Ramon Novarro, and **Min and Bill**.*

*With his bulldog perched behind him, the drama critic of the **New York Telegram**, Robert Garland, poses glumly with his 1930 Packard Model 733 roadster.*

Al Simmons, the great major league outfielder, shows off his 1930 Packard Custom Eight convertible coupe. Born Aloysius Szymanski, he played from 1924 to 1944, most of the time with the Philadelphia Athletics in the American League. Simmons had a lifetime average of .334 and was inducted into the National Baseball Hall of Fame in 1953, three years before his death.

Tom Mix, cowboy star of Hollywood silents and early talking pictures, poses with his famous horse Tony and a 1930 Nash sedan. Born in Mix Run, Pennsylvania in 1880, he made his first film in 1910. After signing with Fox in 1917, he won quick fame as Hollywood's premiere cowboy star.

Actress Dolores Del Rio loved luxury cars. She appears in the book for the third time, with her custom-built 1930 Cadillac V-8 town car. The photograph was taken outside the studio sound stage where she was filming **The Bad One.**

Film star Walter Pidgeon is shown with his 1930 Cadillac V-8 with its unusual spotlight mounted on the radiator. Born in New Brunswick, Canada, in 1897, he has appeared in more than 100 motion pictures since 1926, and has starred in many television shows. Among his many memorable films are **Saratoga** in 1937, **How Green Was My Valley** in 1941, **Mrs. Miniver** in 1942, **Madame Curie** in 1943 and **Executive Suite** in 1954.

Ernst Lubitsch, Paramount's leading producer, is about to enter his chauffeur-driven 1930 Cadillac Fleetwood V-8. Born in Berlin, he got his stage training under Max Reinhardt. He starred Pola Negri in **Madame DuBarry** in 1918 (shown as **Passion** in this country). Two of his best remembered films are **The Merry Widow** in 1934, with Jeannette MacDonald and Maurice Chevalier, and **Ninotchka**, starring Greta Garbo and Melvyn Douglas. He died in 1947 at fifty-five.

The famous Hollywood film director Frank Borzage bids his wife goodbye as their 1930 Cadillac V-16 town car prepares to leave their palatial home for a short trip. Borzage directed forty-nine motion pictures from 1920 to 1959, including **Humoresque** in 1920, **A Farewell to Arms** in 1932, **Disputed Passage** in 1939 and **Smilin' Through** in 1941. He also was the producer of six films. Cadillac was the first to offer a sixteen-cylinder engine, introduced in 1930 and carried through the 1940 model year. Marmon built a V-16 in 1931.

Film actress Constance Bennett was as sophisticated in her tastes in automobiles as she was in the roles she played on the screen. She is pictured here with her 1930 Cadillac V-16 roadster in front of her home. The daughter of matinee idol Richard Bennett and sister of actresses Joan and Barbara Bennett, she appeared in many silent and talking pictures. Many readers will remember her in the **Topper** films. Her five husbands included actor Gilbert Roland.

Two sixteen-cylinder Cadillacs in the family, and both gifts! George Hill, MGM director, bought his wife, author Frances Marion, a new 1930 Cadillac Imperial limousine. A few days later it was his birthday, and she surprised him with the gift of a V-16 convertible coupe. She wrote the screenplays for **The Big House** and **Min and Bill**, both directed by Hill. She also wrote many great film stories directed by Cecil B. DeMille, including **The Ten Commandments**.

The distinguished opera star, Madame Ernestine Schumann-Heink, owned two Cadillac V-16s. She is standing near a 1931 town car, with a 1930 limousine parked behind. The picture was taken in Southern California, presumably at her stately home.

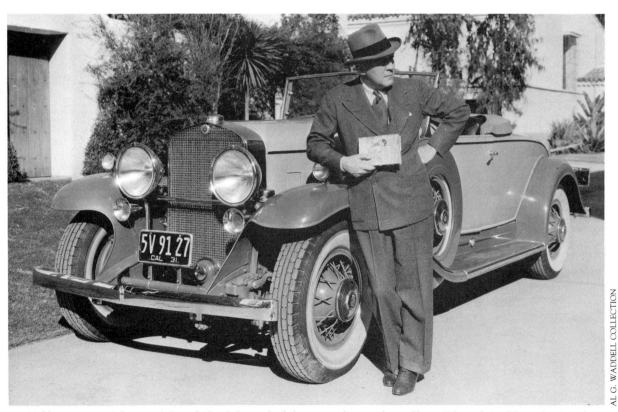

Holding a copy of the novel **Grand Hotel** from which he was making a classic film is Edmund Goulding, the British director who made Hollywood his home. He stands by his 1931 Cadillac V-12 convertible coupe. Among his other great films were **Dark Victory** in 1939 and **The Razor's Edge** in 1946. A few months after introduction of the V-16 in 1930, Cadillac also began offering a V-12.

Arriving for work at the Warner Brothers studio in Hollywood is the famed wide-mouthed comedian Joe E. Brown, at the wheel of a classic 1931 Duesenberg phaeton with a Derham body. Before coming to Hollywood, Brown had a background in circus, vaudeville and basketball. Among many of his remembered films are **Sit Tight** in 1931, **You Said a Mouthful** in 1932, **Show Boat** (as Cap'n Andy) in 1951 and **Some Like It Hot** in 1959. This unusual photograph was taken for Vogue Rubber Company and was in the D. Cameron Peck Collection donated in the 1950s to the Detroit Public Library.

Tyrone Power, one of Hollywood's most popular stars in the late 1930s and early 1940s, owned this 1931 Duesenberg. Born in Cincinnati in 1913, the son of matinee idol Tyrone Power, Sr., he starred in a number of epics including **Lloyds of London** in 1937, **Marie Antoinette** in 1938, **Jesse James** in 1939 and **Johnny Apollo** and **The Mark of Zorro** in 1940. He died of a heart attack in 1958 in Madrid while filming **Solomon and Sheba**.

Photographed in Oakland, California with a new 1931 DeVaux sedan are Norman DeVaux (right), president, and Elbert J. Hall, vice-president in charge of engineering of the DeVaux-Hall Motors Corporation of Grand Rapids, Michigan. The DeVaux was an attractive economy car with a six-cylinder engine which failed after only fourteen months in business. Its assets were taken over by Continental Motor Car Company of Detroit which marketed a similar automobile called the Continental in 1933 and 1934.

Abe Lyman, the orchestra leader, bought this beautiful Packard roadster from Thompson Motor Company in Beverly Hills, California, in the spring of 1931. He hands a check for payment to M. T. Wilhoyte, salesman for the Packard dealership.

Carman Barnes, identified in a publicity release as "the schoolgirl author recently signed to a stellar contract by Paramount," poses with a new 1931 Buick sedan.

*Actress Helen Twelvetrees was filming **Painted Desert** when this photograph of her with a 1931 Chrysler dual-cowl phaeton was taken. Her real name was Helen Jurgens. She appeared in twenty-two movies from 1929 to 1938.*

In this photograph taken in New York's Central Park in early spring of 1931, Fred Astaire seems more interested in the older 1915 Franklin roadster than in the stylish 1931 Franklin sedan behind it. Astaire was starring on Broadway and had yet to appear in the first of many classic Hollywood musicals he made beginning in 1933.

Pictured with a 1931 Bugatti Type GP51 race car is Louis Chiron, described years later by Rodney Walkerley as "an exuberant, Gallic, bubbling, audience-loving character with a blazing excitement over motor racing as an art." Born in Monaco, he won nearly thirty races before World War II, including the French Grand Prix in 1934 and 1935. He raced Talbots, Alfa Romeos and Mercedes as well as Bugattis. During the war he chauffeured generals in staff cars. Bugatti cars were built, never in volume, in Molsheim, France from 1909 to 1956.

*Maurice Chevalier, the inimitable French singing entertainer, was photographed in 1932 with this Bugatti, built about a year earlier. Known throughout the world for his soft accent and handsome smile, he was given a special Academy Award in 1958 "for his contributions to the world of entertainment for more than half a century." He entertained in cabarets, on the stage, in films and on radio and television. One of his best-remembered pictures was **Gigi** in 1958. Chevalier died in 1972 at eighty-four.*

*One of the most popular leading men of the silent screen in Hollywood, Bert Lytell, sits proudly in his 1931 Buick Straight Eight roadster. Two of his memorable films are **To Have and to Hold** in 1917 and **Lady Windermere's Fan** in 1925.*

*Jack Holt, popular Columbia Pictures star, was photographed in his 1931 Packard Custom Eight phaeton on location for his newest picture, **Fifty Fathoms Deep**.*

Paul Whiteman, the distinguished orchestra leader, poses with his baton and his elegant 1931 Cadillac V-16. Whiteman, whose orchestra had for its theme song one of the most beautiful pieces ever written — George Gershwin's "Rhapsody in Blue" — played on Broadway, in Hollywood, in theaters and at the usual one-night stands at colleges and special events during the golden years of the big bands.

Lew Cody, the smartly-dressed leading man of the silent screen, poses with his 1931 Cadillac V-12 outside a movie sound stage. His French accent affected his career in talking pictures although he made two in 1931, **Dishonored** and **Sporting Blood**. He died at fifty in 1934.

Billy Arnold stands on the running board of the 1931 Chrysler Imperial LeBaron roadster in which he set an open-car speed record at Daytona Beach in the spring of 1931. Arnold won the Indianapolis 500 race in 1930, with an average speed of 100.448 miles per hour.

Actress and dancer Lina Basquette autographed this picture of herself with her 1931 DeSoto convertible coupe. As a child ballerina, she was featured in the 1915 San Francisco World's Fair, then was signed by Universal to star in a series of shorts and to play child roles in films. Her most important screen role as an adult was the lead in Cecil B. DeMille's **The Godless Girl** *in 1929. The DeSoto was introduced by Chrysler Corporation in 1928 as a medium-priced car. Its last year was 1961.*

A noted aviation pioneer, Navy Lieut. Walter Hinton (fourth from left) was greeted in Palo Alto, California by Exchange Club members who escorted him to their meeting in this 1931 Packard Custom Eight sedan. Hinton was one of two pilots of the Navy's NC-4 that was the first aircraft to cross the Atlantic in 1918. Six men were aboard as the frail airship made a perfect hop of 800 miles from the Azores to Lisbon.

MGM star Anita Page appears again, this time with a classic 1931 Chrysler Imperial Eight convertible coupe. Films in which she appeared later in the decade included **Justice for Sale** *in 1932,* **The Big Cage** *in 1933 and* **Hitch Hike to Heaven** *in 1936.*

Ohio's Governor George White is seated behind the driver of this 1931 Chrysler Imperial close-coupled four-passenger phaeton, with a custom LeBaron body. The occasion was the first inauguration of White, whose home was in Marietta. He served two terms, from 1931 to 1935. Previously he had been a Congressman for three terms, and in 1920 and 1921 he was chairman of the Democratic National Committee. Driver of the car is James W. Watson, who in a long career in the auto industry held key sales positions with Franklin, Chrysler, Nash and American Motors.

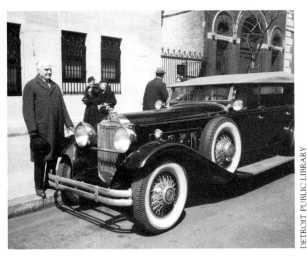

Many Americans living today can credit much of what they know about classical music to the network radio concerts they listened to while in grade or high school anytime from 1928 to 1942. The concerts were conducted by Dr. Walter J. Damrosch, pictured here with his 1931 Packard Custom Eight phaeton. Born in Prussia in 1862, he came to America in 1871. He served as director of the New York Symphony Orchestra from 1903 to 1927 and was musical counsel for the National Broadcasting Company from 1928 to 1947. He died in 1950.

Three opera stars were photographed with this 1931 Pierce-Arrow convertible coupe in the Los Angeles area. From the left, they are Tito Schipa, Margherita Salvi and Richard Bonelli, all of the Chicago Opera.

Forty Packard automobiles carried Wiley Post and Harold Gatty and the official party in the ovation parade up Broadway in New York City the day after the round-the-world fliers ended their epochal flight of 15,474 miles in eight days, fifteen hours, fifty-one minutes. The time was the summer of 1931, and Post and Gatty can be seen sitting on the lowered top of the lead car.

Pioneer aviator Frank Hawks is pictured with his 1931 Franklin convertible speedster with a custom Dietrich body and his famed Travel Air monoplane with which he set a coast-to-coast speed record in 1929. He flew from Los Angeles to New York in twelve hours twenty-five minutes three seconds. A year later he completed the first trans-continental glider flight, towed behind an airplane. He took off from San Diego March 29 and landed in New York April 6. Total elapsed time was thirty-six hours forty-seven minutes.

At the wheel of a big, powerful 1931 Pierce-Arrow five-passenger tourer is the mayor of Syracuse, New York, Rolland J. Marvin. The picture was taken in front of a dealership selling Studebaker, Pierce-Arrow and Rockne cars.

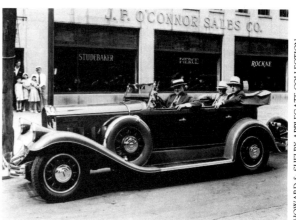

Standing beside a 1931 Studebaker Eight sedan are noted prizefighters W. L. "Young" Stribling and Jack Dempsey. The original publicity picture released by Studebaker does not carry an explanation of the monoplane in the background, with the two women waiting at the right.

He was governor of New York state when this picture was snapped of Franklin D. Roosevelt (fourth from left), behind a 1931 Packard Twin Six sport phaeton. Not many photographs of Roosevelt standing were taken during his long career in politics.

An unusual speed record was made in February 1931 by the veteran automobile test driver, E. G. "Cannon Ball" Baker. He drove this Chrysler Imperial, towing a Plymouth roadster, from Columbus to Marietta, Ohio, in the record elapsed time of one hour and fifty-seven and a half minutes, beating his previous solo record set in 1928 in a Franklin. At the wheel of the open Plymouth is James W. Watson, sales manager of the Chrysler distributorship in Columbus. Standing (from the left): J. G. Young, of the Columbus Chamber of Commerce, and Ernest W. Pavey, Columbus realtor.

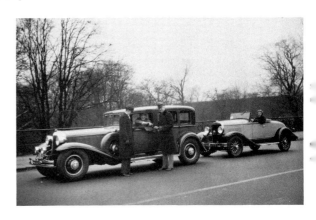

At the wheel of a 1931 Chevrolet sport roadster is Harry Hershfield, a syndicated cartoonist who created the humorous character Abe Kabibble.

142

One of the most beautiful American cars was the Reo Royale, introduced in the 1931 model year. The first Royale delivered anywhere was this five-passenger victoria, which went to Charles M. Toms (right), a banker in Lansing, Michigan, who previously had bought sixteen Reo passenger cars. It was delivered in person in the fall of 1930 by R. H. Scott (left), president, and William Robert Wilson (center), general manager of Reo Motor Car Company of Lansing. The Royale was styled by Alexis de Sakhnoffsky.

A closer look at the classic Reo Royale design. Pictured is a 1932 rumble-seat coupe.

When the new Essex Terraplane line of cars was introduced in mid-1932, Hudson Motor Car Company invited aviation heroine Amelia Earhart to Detroit to make the formal christening before Hudson and Essex dealers. She posed later with several of the low-priced models, including this sedan. It was in 1932 that Amelia Earhart became the first woman to fly across the Atlantic alone, in a Lockheed Vega. Three years later she flew nonstop from Honolulu to California, again alone.

Another distinguished guest at the national dealer meeting in Detroit announcing the 1932 Essex Terraplane was aviation pioneer Orville Wright, shown with the coupe presented to him by the Hudson Motor Car Company. With his brother Wilbur, he was the first to fly a heavier-than-air machine at Kitty Hawk, North Carolina on December 17, 1903. The Essex Terraplane succeeded the low-priced Essex produced by Hudson Motor Car Company since 1919. In fourteen years, more than 1,300,000 Essex passenger cars were built.

Garfield Arthur "Gar" Wood, named for the American president and vice-president who were inaugurated the year he was born in Mapleton, Iowa, stands beside his 1932 Essex Terraplane sedan. Known as the Gray Fox of Algonac, Wood invented the hydraulic hoist for motor trucks, developed what became the hit-and-run PT boat of World War II, financed the company that built Chris-Craft boats and became one of the immortals of motor boat racing. He won four Gold Cups and was the first victor for the United States of the Harmsworth British International Trophy, which he successfully defended seven times. He died in 1971 at ninety.

Power-boat enthusiasts and pilots Horace E. Dodge, Jr. (left) and Kaye Don also like the 1932 Essex Terraplane convertible coupe. Bodies for the low-priced open models were made in Detroit by Briggs.

Pictured with a 1932 Rockne Six 75 convertible roadster is Anita Louise, who appeared in many movies between 1929 and 1952. She was filming **The Phantom of Crestwood** when this photograph was taken. The Rockne, offered only in 1932 and 1933, was built in Detroit by Rockne Motors Corporation, a Studebaker company. It was named for Knute Rockne, Notre Dame football coach who died in an airplane crash.

This unusual photograph of the notorious murderer and robber, Clyde Barrow, with his arsenal and a 1932 Ford V-8 convertible sedan was made from one of six negatives found in a gunman's rendezvous in a Joplin, Missouri suburb on April 13, 1933, after two officers had been slain when two men and two women shot their way out of a police trap. It is likely that the Ford car shown is the one he stole in Temple, Texas on December 23, 1932. After a series of senseless killings of innocent people over a period of years, in consort with Bonnie Parker, Barrow himself was killed by a Louisiana posse in May 1934.

Photographed at the entrance to Studebaker Corporation are D. Absalom Jenkins (better known as Ab), and Albert R. Erskine, Studebaker president, with a 1932 Pierce-Arrow custom-bodied roadster. Jenkins ran a twelve-cylinder Pierce-Arrow for twenty-four hours at Bonneville in Utah for an average speed of 112.935 mph, on September 18 and 19, 1932. Once the mayor of Salt Lake City, he shattered more than sixty speed records in his career, many of them for Studebaker, which controlled Pierce-Arrow from 1928 to 1933.

Members of the famous "Our Gang" comedy group sat still long enough to have their pictures taken with a 1932 Studebaker President St. Regis brougham.

Film actress Madge Evans loved Packard automobiles, especially 1932 models. She is pictured here with three of them. Her first motion picture was a silent, **Classmates,** made in 1924. She appeared in thirty-seven films in all, the last in 1938. Two of her most memorable pictures were **Dinner at Eight** in 1933 and **David Copperfield** in 1935. Above, she enters a 1932 Packard Eight DeLuxe all-weather cabriolet.

Madge Evans takes a 1932 Packard Eight DeLuxe convertible coupe to a fashionable Hollywood golf course.

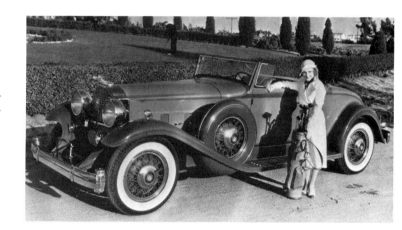

She takes this handsome 1932 Packard Eight two-passenger coupe when she goes shopping.

148

Popular radio and screen comedian Joe Penner, whose line "Wanna buy a duck?" always drew laughs, stands with his wife by their elegant 1932 Packard DeLuxe Eight convertible victoria. He appeared in several motion pictures, including **College Rhythm** *in 1934,* **I'm From the City** *in 1938 and* **Millionaire Playboy** *in 1940.*

To stimulate circulation, newspapers in major American cities often engaged the services of prominent home economists to put on cooking schools in local communities. Jessie DeBoth, shown here with a 1932 Pontiac Six, was one of them. A Pontiac publicist persuaded her to comment on the new car. "It's smart, comfortable and easy to handle," she was quoted as saying in a national news release.

The Queen Mother of the Netherlands, Queen Wilhelmina (back seat, left), was favorably impressed with the riding qualities of the Mercedes-Benz eight-cylinder car, type Nurburg, which she used during her stay in Freudenstadt, Germany, in 1932. That, according to the caption for this picture, released at the time by Daimler-Benz.

149

Dick Powell was at the height of his film career when this photograph was taken of him standing leisurely in front of his Hollywood home. His beautiful 1932 Packard Standard Eight convertible victoria is parked in the driveway. Powell made sixty movies from 1931 to 1954, most of them with happy themes.

Standing beside a 1932 Packard Twin Six special-bodied sedan limousine is Sir MacPherson Robertson, sponsor of the London-to-Melbourne air race, for which he gave the gold cup valued then at £650. A great air enthusiast, he was the largest candy manufacturer in Australia.

Charles W. Nash (right), chairman of Nash Motors, was on hand when an "official guest" car, a 1932 Nash sedan, was delivered to the mayor of Chicago, Anton J. Cermak. Less than a year later Cermak was killed by a would-be assassin of President-elect Franklin D. Roosevelt in Florida.

*Oliver Hardy and Stan Laurel are seen again, with Hardy telling Laurel who will drive the 1932 Studebaker Commander Regal sedan. They were making **Their First Mistake** when this photograph was taken. Born in Britain, Laurel made seventy-six films before teaming with Hardy in 1927. He had a wide array of mannerisms that endeared him to audiences including a baby-like weep, a confused eye blink and a bewildered scratching of the top of his head. Hardy, who liked to believe he was the unquestioned leader of the two, professed intelligence he obviously lacked.*

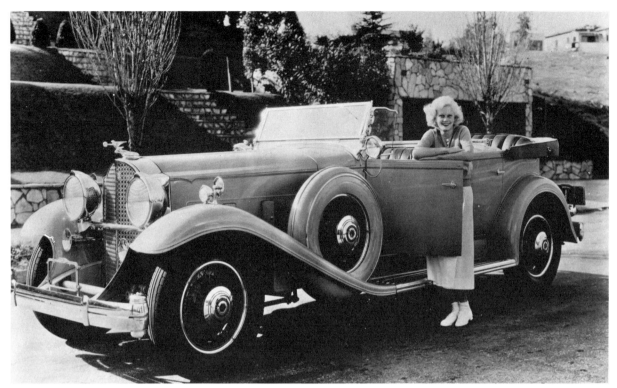

*Pictured with her 1932 Packard Twin Six is film actress Jean Harlow, who in a short career left an indelible mark on American motion pictures. Born Harlean Carpenter in Kansas City in 1911, she starred first in **Hell's Angels**, produced in 1927. But it was not until she signed a contract with MGM that her talents were generally recognized. Among her most noted films was **Platinum Blonde** in 1931.*

At the wheel of a sleek new 1932 Packard Twin Six phaeton is Tommy Milton, the first two-time winner of the Indianapolis 500 race. He drove a Frontenac to victory in 1921 and an HCS Special in 1923. Milton is remembered also for setting a one-mile straightaway speed record of 156 miles per hour in a Duesenberg at Daytona Beach in 1920.

Golfer Gene Sarazen was photographed in 1932 with two different Packard Twin Six convertible sedans. Wearing his golfing knickers, he steps into a model with the standard Packard body (above). Note the one-piece windshield and whitewall tires. Pictured with his wife and Alvan Macauley, Packard president, he is shown below with his very own "Individual Custom Convertible Sedan," with a custom Dietrich body.

Photographed with their new 1932 Packard, purchased from the Packard dealer in Flushing, New York, are the famous magician Howard Thurston and his wife.

Ted Weems (right), the orchestra leader, took delivery of a 1932 Packard Twin Six sport phaeton on June 15, 1932. With him is the salesman, Charlie Crowl, of the Packard branch in Chicago. Weems had one of the most consistently successful dance bands of the 1930s and 1940s.

Edsel Ford, president of Ford Motor Company, drove this beautiful Lincoln roadster as the pace car at the Indianapolis 500-mile race on Memorial Day 1932. The car had a custom body by Murphy.

Hollywood actress Sylvia Sidney was filming **Merrily We Go to Hell** *when this photograph of her with a 1932 Lincoln was taken. The question is, did she travel in this beautiful car with its custom Judkins body? Sylvia Sidney appeared in twenty-nine motion pictures from 1929 to 1955.*

In the heyday of network radio, one of the leading stars was Phillips H. Lord, who created the homespun characters of "Seth Parker" and "Country Doctor." He liked open cars, especially this 1932 Packard Standard Eight convertible coupe, with its custom Brewster body.

In his new capacity as "highway safety adviser" for Plymouth, Barney Oldfield, the internationally-known race driver, helped publicize the 1933 Plymouth. He was host at Plymouth's exhibits at major auto shows across the country. Oldfield told the author during the Automotive Golden Jubilee in Detroit in 1946 that "it isn't easy to smile with a cigar in my mouth, but I try."

A comedian well known to an America deep in its worst economic depression, Herman Timberg (left), takes delivery of this elegant 1932 Packard Eight deluxe sport sedan. A salesman for Packard-Minneapolis made the sale.

Behind the wheel of his new 1932 Packard Light Eight five-passenger sedan is Heartley "Hunk" Anderson, who succeeded Knute Rockne as coach of the Notre Dame football team following Rockne's death in an airplane crash.

Those who remember the Golden Age of Radio will recognize Gary Bonham, one of the Tasty-Yeast Jesters, popular network entertainers. Bonham is shown with his 1932 Packard Light Eight sedan.

Pictured with a 1932 Studebaker President Eight sedan outside a Hollywood sound stage is Una Merkel. A character actress who started in the 1930s as the heroine's-girlfriend type, she later played mothers and aunts. Her many films included **Saratoga** *in 1937,* **Road to Zanzibar** *in 1941 and* **Spinout** *in 1966, with Elvis Presley.*

Pictured with a handsome 1933 Chevrolet sedan are (from the left) Glen S. "Pop" Warner, head football coach at Stanford University, and Andy Kerr, assistant coach. Kerr later was head coach at Washington & Jefferson and Colgate.

A longtime baseball umpire in the American League, George J. Moriarity, stands by his 1933 Chevrolet coupe. As a player from 1903 to 1916, he had a lifetime batting average of .256. He was an umpire from 1917 to 1926, when he resigned to become manager of the Detroit Tigers (in 1927 and 1928), then returned in 1929 to umpiring, his specialty until 1940.

In its second year, the Essex Terraplane, new low-priced car built by the Hudson Motor Car Company in Detroit, was doing well. Roy D. Chapin, shown with a handsome 1933 eight-cylinder convertible coupe, resumed the company presidency that year, after serving in President Herbert Hoover's cabinet as secretary of commerce.

Nancy Witcher (Langhorne) Astor, more familiarly known as Lady Astor, owned this six-cylinder Essex Terraplane convertible coupe in 1933. The picture was taken at her home, Clivenden-on-the-Thames, in England. Virginia-born, she married Waldorf Astor in 1906 and was elected in 1919 as the first woman to sit in Parliament. She served as an influential Conservative member until 1945.

Phillips H. Lord, the radio personality, also liked the 1933 Essex Terraplane convertible coupe. In fact, he bought this peppy little eight-cylinder car. The small inset photo shows him as Seth Parker.

Dressed in evening clothes, actor Gene Raymond prepares to go to a Hollywood formal dinner party in a 1933 Buick sedan. He was born Raymond Guion in New York City and made his acting debut on Broadway in 1920. He entered films in the 1930s, changing his name to Gene Raymond. He made six films in 1933, including **Zoo in Budapest** *and* **Flying Down to Rio.** *Raymond married Jeanette MacDonald in 1937.*

Frank "King" Clancy, associated for decades with the Toronto Maple Leafs as coach and general manager of the National Hockey League club, was photographed with his 1933 Packard Light Eight convertible coupe, on March 17, 1933. The original picture was taken by Pringle & Booth Limited, Toronto.

The distinguished owner of this 1933 Packard Eight coupe roadster was Mlle. Camille Vierpont, of Casablanca, Morocco.

*A salesman shows film actress Leila Hyams a 1933 Packard Twelve. She made thirty-four pictures from 1924 to 1936, including **Island of Lost Souls, Sing Sinner Sing** and **Saturday's Millions** — all in 1933.*

Here are two photographs of the same Mercedes-Benz SS cabriolet owned by actress Lillian Harvey, taken about five years apart. The top picture was made in 1933 soon after she bought the elegant car. She had just finished filming the German movie, **Ich und die Kaiserin,** and was soon to return to Hollywood to complete two additional 1933 films, **My Weakness** and **My Lips Betray.**

The bottom photo shows Miss Harvey at her home outside Elstree, England, sitting on the front fender of the Mercedes. She had started to film **Invitation to the Waltz,** her first starring British picture, released in 1938. The talented actress from 1928 to 1940 appeared in twenty-five movies, eleven of them in German, thirteen in English and one in French.

President Franklin D. Roosevelt, despite his infantile paralysis, liked to drive his 1933 DeSoto. The photograph, taken at Warm Springs, Georgia, shows him getting out of the car as his Secretary of Labor, Frances Perkins, waits.

163

This 1933 Grosser Mercedes MB, a gift from Adolf Hitler, served Emperor Hirohito of Japan well into the 1950s. As the owner of this interesting photograph, Hendrik Kranendonk of Muiderberg, Netherlands, observes: "Although nowadays we are swamped with Japanese cars, before and long after World War II they did not build anything worthy of their emperor." The picture was taken in the late 1950s at the Tokyo airport. With Hirohito is a visiting head of state, the president of India.

The celebrated tenor, Lauritz Melchior, is pictured with his wife and their 1933 Packard Twelve sedan at their summer estate near Chossewitz, Germany, where Melchior had a 3,000-acre hunting preserve. Born in Copenhagen in 1890, he sang Tannhäuser at his first appearance with the Metropolitan Opera in 1926. He remained on its roster until 1950, three years after becoming an American citizen. Melchior died in 1973.

About to enter her 1933 Humber Pullman landaulette is Britain's Queen Elizabeth, mother of the present reigning Queen Elizabeth. The Humber has been built in England since 1898.

*The incomparable comedian W. C. Fields stands rather lethargically by his 1933 Lincoln V-12 LeBaron convertible roadster. Born William Claude Dukenfield in Philadelphia in 1879, he appeared in his first Broadway play, **The Ham Tree,** in 1905. His first film was **Pool Sharks** in 1915, but he did not make another picture for a decade. Fields starred in every version of the Ziegfeld Follies from 1915 to 1921, and really came into his own when sound came to motion pictures. He wrote the screenplays for many of his films, using such improbable pseudonyms as Otis J. Criblecoblis and Charles Bogle. He died in 1946.*

As crowds look on, the Grand Duchesse of Luxembourg passes by in a 1933 Studebaker convertible sedan.

The nation's first lady, Eleanor Roosevelt, had her favorite car, too — a 1933 Plymouth convertible coupe.

Opening the door of his 1933 Buick sedan is Wiley Post, the noted American aviator, In 1931 he flew with Harold Gatty around the northern part of the earth (15,474 miles in eight days, fifteen hours and fifty-one minutes. This photograph was taken soon after he made somewhat the same trip alone, traveling 15,596 miles in a few minutes less than seven days, nineteen hours. Included was a non-stop hop from Brooklyn to Berlin. Post was killed in 1935 in an airplane crash near Point Barrow, Alaska, while on a flight with Will Rogers, his passenger.

Packards led the cortege for the funeral of Wiley Post in
California on August 22, 1935.

Two baseball stars with the 1934 pennant-winning Detroit Tigers look over a new Dodge sedan. They are
Pete Fox, at the wheel, and Lynwood "Schoolboy" Rowe. Fox, an outfielder, played with Detroit and Boston in the
American League from 1933 to 1945. Rowe had a fabulous record as a Detroit pitcher in 1934, winning twenty-four
while losing only eight.

When Carl Brisson, the Danish-born singing and dancing star, was photographed in this 1934
*Isotta-Fraschini, he was filming **Murder at the Vanities** in Hollywood. He earlier had starred in two British silent films*
directed by Alfred Hitchcock. The Isotta-Fraschini, long recognized as one of Italy's finest cars, was built in Milan for
half a century, from 1899 to 1949.

167

When film actor Chester Morris was relaxing with his *1934 Buick sedan*, he was between two pictures — **Let's Talk It Over** and **The Gay Bride,** both made in 1934. Morris almost always played a determined two-fisted hero. He portrayed Boston Blackie in thirteen of the series' action films.

His young son sitting on the running board, the Sultan of Langkat poses proudly with his 1934 Packard Twelve convertible sedan. Langkat then was a district of Sumatra.

A 1934 Packard Twelve town car with a custom Rollston body was delivered to Thomas Sollowey (with cane), a wealthy Canadian gold mining company executive, who paid $10,000 for it. The happy salesman was Bill Thomas (right), of Packard's New York Branch. The picture was taken by John Adams Davis, noted automobile photographer of the period.

This elegant 1934 Packard Twelve convertible victoria, with its special LeBaron custom body, was owned by Ricardo LaCosta, Jr., a leading attorney of Puerto Rico, at the wheel.

The prime minister of Egypt, Abdel-Fattah Pasha Yehla, is about to enter his official automobile, a 1934 Packard Twelve limousine. The photograph was taken December 6, 1934.

On the back of this original photograph, found in the Packard Motor Car Company files, is the notation that the dignitary shown with his 1934 Packard Super Eight touring car is "His Highness, the Ruler of Sandur State, India."

*This striking photograph of a 1934 Packard Super Eight convertible victoria features Hazel Forbes, who won fame in the Ziegfeld Follies. She appeared in one Hollywood film, **Down to Their Last Yacht**, produced in 1934.*

Posing almost casually with his 1934 Packard Eight convertible victoria is Captain Ingamar A. Theodoru, of Bucharest, Roumania. That's his home in the background.

Famed radio newscaster Lowell Thomas traveled to Detroit in 1934 to take delivery of a new Hudson sedan. Every weekday evening for several decades Thomas presented a fifteen-minute network news report on happenings around the world. He also was a noted world traveler, and in a long and eventful lifetime interviewed some of the most important figures of the twentieth century.

With her 1934 Packard Eight sedan is Norma Shearer, one of the great Hollywood actresses who starred in both silent and talking pictures. She won an Academy Award as best actress in 1929 for **The Divorcee.** *When this photograph was taken, she was filming the memorable* **Barrets of Wimpole Street.**

This photograph of Hollywood actress Arline Judge is different from most because it not only shows her car, a 1934 Packard Eight coupe roadster, but also the palatial home that goes with it. She was in films for two decades starting with **Bachelor Apartment** *in 1931. One of her best was* **George White's 1935 Scandals.**

171

Wearing an Indian head-dress is the incomparable Kate Smith, photographed in Sioux City, Iowa on April 25, 1934 with a Studebaker sedan. She was initiated into the Winnebago Tribe with the name "Glory of the Moon." Born Kathryn Elizabeth Smith, the great American singer has had a fabulous career on the stage, in films, on radio and on television. She made her radio debut in 1931 with a program called "Kate Smith Sings." She starred from 1938 to 1951 on "Kate Smith Speaks." She introduced more than 700 songs, including "God Bless America" in 1938. She had her own television show from 1950 to 1954.

Mickey Riley, international swimming champion, is proud of his 1934 Hudson touring sedan.

Hollywood actress Jean Harlow appears again, this time on the running board of her 1934 Cadillac V-12 town car. It was in 1934 that she starred in the classic film **Dinner at Eight**. She died in 1937, during the filming of **Saratoga**, of cerebral edema. She was twenty-six.

The first lady of American musical comedy, Ethel Merman, waves as she prepares to leave a Hollywood studio in her 1934 DeSoto sedan. She was born in Astoria, Queens, New York, in 1909 and became known on Broadway and in films as the owner of one of the most powerful, strident voices in show business. Two pictures she made in 1934, when both Chrysler and DeSoto car models embraced the controversial new Airflow design, were **Kid Millions** and **We're Not Dressing.** Other more famous Merman films were **Stage Door Canteen** in 1943 and **Call Me Madam** in 1953.

Film actress Janet Gaynor is shown in a movie still with a 1934 Ford V-8 coupe. Born Laura Gainor in Philadelphia in 1906, she became a Fox box-office star soon after her work in **Sunrise** in 1927. In 1928 she became the first actress ever to win an Academy Award, for **Seventh Heaven.** She starred with Will Rogers in **State Fair,** a 1933 hit, and won an Oscar nomination in 1937 for her memorable performance in **A Star Is Born.**

Werner Heuer Lares, director of the Venezuelan daily newspaper **El Universal,** stands beside his 1934 Packard Eight sedan limousine, in the driveway of his home in Caracas.

The unidentified man in this picture, taken in the lobby of the Lincoln Hotel in New York, is showing Fro Grimes, singer with Lester Lannin's Orchestra, how to raise the hood on a 1934 Ford convertible coupe.

Dr. Fred N. Bonine, a well-known physician of Niles, Michigan, owned this 1934 LaSalle. The companion car to Cadillac, introduced in 1927, lasted through the 1940 model year.

President Franklin D. Roosevelt is shown riding in an open Packard in a motorcade in Rochester, Minnesota in 1934. He is in the back seat of the second car. Nearest the camera is a Cadillac carrying newsmen.

Fred Waring and his Pennsylvanians was one of the leading orchestras during the big-band era that began in the 1920s and ended soon after the advent of television. For a number of years Waring's band was sponsored on radio by Ford Motor Company. He is shown in the front passenger seat of this 1934 Ford V-8 phaeton.

Clark Gable, one of Hollywood's greatest box-office stars, stands leisurely beside his 1935 Duesenberg roadster with its low, sleek custom body by Bohman & Schwartz, coach builders of Pasadena, California. A year earlier he received an Academy Award for best actor in **It Happened One Night.** Some of his other best-remembered films are **Strange Interlude** in 1932, **Mutiny on the Bounty** in 1939, **Gone With The Wind** in 1939, **Boom Town** in 1940 and **The Tall Men** in 1955. He died in 1960 at fifty-nine.

The internationally-celebrated entertainer, Josephine Baker, is as smartly dressed as her 1935 Delage. Born in St. Louis in 1906, she started her career at eight, singing in Harlem nightclubs. After a few years as a Broadway chorine, she went to Paris where she became a legend and commanded the highest pay of any entertainer in Europe. She appeared in numerous French films and was decorated by the French government for her activities as an entertainer and an ambulance driver in World War II. She died in 1975. The highly-regarded Delage was produced in France from 1905 to 1954.

*Stepping into his classic 1935 Lincoln convertible sedan with its custom LeBaron body is film actor Norman Foster. Born Norman Hoeffer in 1900, he made his Broadway debut in 1926. On stage and in many Hollywood motion pictures, he played light leads. Foster turned to directing in 1936 for Fox. He directed the Mr. Moto and Charlie Chan films. Later he starred in such mature Westerns as **Woman on the Run** in 1950 and **Navajo** in 1952. His former wives included Claudette Colbert and Sally Blane.*

176

Standing on the running board of his 1935 Studebaker sedan (to appear taller, of course) is the irrepressible Mickey Rooney. On stage from the age of two, when he was known by his real name, Joe Yule, he has been an outstanding star ever since on the stage, in films, on radio and on television. He took the name Mickey Rooney in 1932. Well known for his Andy Hardy pictures and his teaming with Judy Garland, he starred in **Boys Town** in 1938, **Babes in Arms** in 1939 and **The Human Comedy** in 1943. Mickey starred in the television series **Hey Mulligan** in 1954 and **Mickey** in 1964.

Maryland's Governor Harry W. Nice, shown with Mrs. Nice standing beside their 1935 Packard Twelve sedan, loved to tour by automobile. They visited all forty-eight states and most of Canada by car.

The distinguished Belgian, Prince Eugene de Ligne, a noted sportsman of the time, owned a 1935 Packard Eight convertible victoria.

177

*In an attempt to develop for its new low-priced 1935 One Twenty series the same prestige as its traditional more expensive luxury models, Packard engaged the famed Metropolitan Opera singer Lawrence Tibbett to help publicize the all-new car. He appeared in the Twentieth Century Fox film, **Metropolitan,** driving this One Twenty convertible coupe. This photograph also highlighted a full-page ad in **Fortune,** which carefully pointed out that Mr. Tibbett "for his own personal motor car" owned a Packard Twelve.*

The nattily-attired Italian ambassador to the United States, Augusto Rosso, poses with his 1935 Packard Twelve. The picture was taken on the grounds of the Ambassador Hotel in Los Angeles.

Amelia Earhart, the noted aviatrix, was on hand as a guest at the Indianapolis 500 Mile Race in 1935. She is seated in the Ford phaeton that paced the event that year, driven by Harry Mack, Ford's Detroit district sales manager.

*A 1935 Packard Eight convertible shares the spotlight in the 1939 Paramount film **Some Like It Hot.**
In this movie still, Shirley Ross and Bernard Nedell discuss who will drive. A former band vocalist, Miss Ross starred in light Hollywood films of the 1930s and early 1940s, several with Bob Hope. She will be remembered for her role in the 1936 picture **San Francisco.***

Actress Patricia Ellis made thirty-four movies from 1932 to 1939 — seven of them in 1935, when this Hudson Six convertible coupe was all the rage. The full retail price for the car was $790. This photograph was taken in Detroit in February 1935.

Raymond C. Moley (left), political economist from Ohio who was the central figure in President Franklin D. Roosevelt's "Brain Trust" during his first administration, accepts the keys to his new 1935 Packard Eight coupe from Alvan Macauley, Packard president.

A prominent Philadelphia physician, Dr. Nathaniel W. Boyd, prepares to enter his 1935 Packard One Twenty sedan.

*Entering his chauffeur-driven 1935 Packard Twelve is Harold Lloyd, the bespectacled comedian who starred
in hundreds of motion pictures, both silent and talking, beginning with two-reelers in 1916. Lloyd was presented
with a special Academy Award in 1952 as "master comedian and good citizen."*

*Bohman & Schwartz, successor to Murphy, built the custom body for this 1935 Duesenberg SJ for
Prince Alexis Mdivani, who married Barbara Hutton just before she inherited twenty million dollars. He died
soon after this picture was taken.*

181

A leading businessman from Davenport, Iowa, H. C. Simmons, president of Hansen Engineering Company, was so proud of his 1935 Packard One Twenty coupe that he had this picture taken and sent it to the editor of the company magazine, **The Inner Circle.**

Elliott Roosevelt, son of President Franklin D. Roosevelt, and his wife take delivery of their 1935 Packard One Twenty convertible at the factory in Detroit.

A 1935 Lincoln stars with Melvyn Douglas and Claudette Colbert in the Columbia picture, **She Married Her Boss.** Douglas, born Melvyn Hesselberg in Macon, Georgia in 1901, was a popular film star of the 1930s and 1940s. He played Greta Garbo's leading man in **As You Desire Me** in 1932, and in 1963 won an Academy Award as the best supporting actor in **Hud.** Miss Colbert was born in Paris in 1905 as Claudette Lily Chauchoin. She made her screen debut in 1927. A perennial motion picture favorite, she earned an Oscar as best actress in 1934, in the classic **It Happened One Night.**

1936-1945: *A Turn to War*

When Americans viewed the glittering new 1936 cars — which included such fascinating newcomers as the imaginative Cord 810 — they had little notion that their nation within six years would become irretrievably embroiled in a horrendous global war. But the signs were there. A blustering Italian dictator named Mussolini conquered the ancient kingdom of Ethiopia, and a strutting fanatic named Hitler boasted that he had fulfilled his promise to restore military might to the Fatherland. As the theater newsreels recorded the discovery that the revolt against the Spanish Republic was gaining support from Germany and Italy, the average American found the idea that these remote developments could lead to a world war utterly preposterous.

Meanwhile, back on the auto front, the manufacturers with a wide array of new models, new features and technical advances were slowly leading the country out of the long depression. By 1936 more than half of all U.S. families owned automobiles, with a good portion of the models having been bought used. The Automobile Manufacturers Association reported that ninety-five per cent of all cars built in 1936 had dealer prices below $750. Designers were learning to form steel with the same high degree of imagination and skill that they had applied to the wooden bodies so long in vogue. In the years before America's total involvement in World War II, automobile buyers savored these developments (not necessarily in order of importance): the battery under the hood instead of beneath the seat, the gearshift lever mounted on the steering column instead of on the floor, attractive two-tone paint combinations, air-conditioning, fresh-air heating systems, sealed-beam headlights, automatic transmissions, disappearance of the running boards and more factory-installed radios than ever before. In 1939 news that the seventy-five millionth U.S.-built car had been produced led some soothsayers to state flatly that the

saturation point for automobiles was at hand.

More roads were being constructed, but experts were warning that existing highways were deteriorating and that with the great increases in travel, automobile accidents were showing startling climbs every year.

Many of the new highways led to new airports that served virtually every city of any size — for the airplane was beginning to be accepted as a more modern way to travel, especially for individuals on business.

America was committed to help its allies as war broke out in Europe, and all auto manufacturers were granted Government contracts to produce a broad variety of war materiel. After the Japanese attack December 7, 1941 on Pearl Harbor, however, the industry quickly earned the title Arsenal of Democracy as it turned all its plants totally to war production. The last U.S. automobiles were built February 9, 1942, and for the duration the industry's personality turned from that of a group of companies engaged in a competitive business to win American consumers to that of an awesomely powerful industrial force whose single purpose was to do its part to help win the war.

DETROIT PUBLIC LIBRARY

America's automobile showrooms fairly glistened with excitement when the new 1937 models bowed. Pictured is the showroom of Packard Philadelphia during Ladies' Week, a national promotion that drew hundreds of thousands to see the new Packard models.

Hollywood actress Gloria Shea sits on the front fender of an attractive 1936 Chevrolet coupe. She appeared in twelve movies, with her first, **Life Begins,** released in 1932. Her last pciture was **One Way Ticket,** in 1936.

Hollywood stars James Stewart and Wendy Barrie are pictured with a 1936 DeSoto convertible coupe on the MGM lot. Born in Indiana, Pennsylvania in 1908, Stewart has played slow-speaking honest heroes for nearly four decades. He won an Academy Award in 1940 as best actor in **The Philadelphia Story** and was nominated for four others. Wendy Barrie was born Wendy Jenkins in Hong Kong in 1912. Educated in England and Switzerland, she made her British screen debut in 1933 as Jane Seymour in **The Private Life of Henry VIII.** Her Hollywood roles rarely did justice to her talents. She had her own television show, "Through Wendy's Window," in 1949 and 1950. She died in 1978.

After completion of the film **Lady Be Careful,** *actor Grant Withers drove to the Paramount lot in this 1936 Ford convertible. He announced that he was partly responsible for the ultra-modern custom streamlining of the car executed by Jensen in England. Withers appeared in sixty-five pictures from 1928 to 1955.*

For getting nearly twenty-three miles per gallon of gasoline with his 1936 Hudson sedan in the Gilmore-Yosemite Economy Run, Wilbur Shaw (left), the famed race driver, received a silver cup trophy from Earle Gilmore, president of Gilmore Oil Company. The annual event was the predecessor of the Mobil Oil Economy Runs that came later.

When this Cord 810 front-drive model came out, it was so strikingly different in design from any car built in the world that it was the center of admiration wherever it went. E. L. Cord, who had built the L-29 series from 1929 to 1932, tried again, but the revolutionary styling while greatly applauded did not sell, and the company failed after only two years. Seated in this 1936 convertible model are Hollywood stars Dick Powell and Joan Blondell.

The ageless comedian Bob Hope is proud of his 1936 Packard Eight convertible victoria. He has been a top star in motion pictures and on radio and television since the 1930s. In addition, millions of American servicemen and service-women will remember his entertaining them at bases all around the world during and since World War II.

Photographed with a 1936 Hudson touring sedan is Sir Malcolm Campbell, British automobile and speedboat racer. On September 3, 1935, he became the first to propel a vehicle on land more than 300 mph. He piloted the **Bluebird,** which he designed, over the Bonneville Salt Flats in Utah at 301.1292 mph. In 1937, on Lake Maggiore near Locarno, Switzerland, he drove a twelve-cylinder boat, also called **Bluebird,** at an average speed of 129.4164 mph, setting a new world record which eclipsed Gar Wood's previous hydroplane mark.

Twentieth Century Fox purchased these two 1936 Packard models for use in films. Accepting the Super Eight sedan and One Twenty convertible coupe is David Butler, the director of nearly all of Shirley Temple's pictures who had just completed work on the film **White Fang.** With Butler is William Simonson, Packard salesman.

One of Hollywood's most successful actresses, Irene Dunne, stands beside her 1936 Packard One Twenty convertible coupe. She made her first Broadway appearance in **The Clinging Vine** in 1922. She was signed to a Hollywood contract by RKO in 1929, and for twenty-two years starred in a variety of roles. She was nominated for best actress in five films including **Cimarron** in 1931 and **The Awful Truth** in 1937. President Eisenhower in 1957 appointed Miss Dunne to be an alternate delegate to the United Nations Twelfth General Assembly.

It hardly resembles a Ford, but it is a 1936 Ford town car with a special Brewster body. Standing demurely at the rear door is its owner, Gladys Swarthout, the popular singing star of radio and Hollywood. She made five films from 1937 to 1939, including **Champagne Waltz** in 1937.

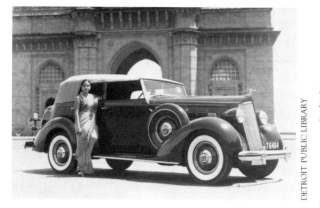

Standing beside her 1936 Packard One Twenty convertible sedan is Miss Rosie, glamorous cinema actress of Imperial Film Company, Bombay, India.

Three men well known to racing and Indianapolis, their homes at the time, posed with game they claimed they shot while hunting in Michigan. With a 1936 Packard 120-B sedan are, from the left: Wilbur Shaw, Wild Bill Cummings and Preston Tucker. Shaw won the Indianapolis 500 race three times (1937, 1939 and 1940), Cummings was the 500 winner in 1934 and Tucker formed a company after World War II to build the ill-fated Tucker car.

*Pictured beside a 1937 Studebaker President sedan is Ken Maynard, a leading cowboy movie star whose riding stunts with his horse Tarzan endeared him to a generation of youngsters. Born in Vevay, Indiana in 1895, he entered films in 1925. Some of his best-remembered pictures are **The Demon Rider** in 1925, **The Red Raiders** in 1927, **The Wagon Master** in 1929 and **Sons of the Saddle** in 1930*

Queen Wilhelmina of the Netherlands holds her hat in a brisk wind as she emerges from the palace "Noordeinde" in the Hague. The 1936 Cadillac awaiting her has a collapsible rear roof section.

Amelia Earhart was photographed in April 1936 with her new Terraplane coupe. She took delivery at the factory in Detroit.

Film star Wallace Beery and his daughter Carol Ann admire the 1936 eleven-passenger Siebert-built Ford sedan bus that Beery used for long-distance travel, hunting and camping. A character star for many years with MGM, he played tough, ugly, slow-thinking and easy-going parts. Some of his best films were **The Last of the Mohicans** *in 1921,* **Casey at the Bat** *in 1927,* **The Big House** *and* **Min and Bill,** *both in 1930, and* **Old Hutch** *and* **A Message to Garcia,** *both in 1936. Beery died at sixty-nine in 1949.*

189

The zany Marx Brothers — Harpo, Chico and Groucho — were photographed with a 1936 Studebaker courtesy car in Cleveland Municipal Stadium on August 2, 1936. Sixty-five thousand fans were on hand to watch their antics, as well as to watch a baseball game between the Cleveland Indians and the first-place New York Yankees. There were two other Marx brothers, Gummo and Zeppo, who appeared with the group in earlier years.

Almost unrecognizable without his heavy makeup, Emmett Kelly, the famous circus clown, stands beside his 1936 Studebaker Dictator coupe. Kelly appeared for years with the Ringling Brothers Barnum & Bailey Circus and was featured in three motion pictures — **The Fat Man** in 1951, **The Greatest Show on Earth** in 1952 and **Wind Across the Everglades** in 1958.

President Franklin D. Roosevelt, riding in a 1936 Packard dual-cowl phaeton, campaigns for re-election to a second term. The photograph was taken in Knoxville, Tennessee.

By 1936, opera star Tito Schipa had moved from a Nash to a Hudson sedan. The Italian tenor made extensive tours of Europe and South America in his career. He appeared in three motion pictures, including the 1940 French film, **Who Is Happier Than I?**

Standing in front of his 1937 Packard 120 touring sedan is Colonel Roscoe Turner, the pioneer aviator who operated his own airfield and flying service in the late 1920s. He set numerous speed records and won the Thompson Trophy Race in 1934. Born in Corinth, Mississippi in 1895, he died in Indianapolis in 1970. Turner was much-honored in America and abroad for his exploits.

In the year in which he starred in **Parnell** and **Saratoga,** Hollywood star Clark Gable took time off to attend the National Air Races in Cleveland. He is pictured with the official staff car, a 1937 Studebaker coupe.

Clark Gable and Myrna Loy stand on the roof of a 1937 Dodge sedan during filming of **Too Hot to Handle,** *a 1938 motion picture. Gable appeared in sixty-eight films from 1931 to 1967, and Miss Loy appeared in eighty-eight from 1926 to 1960.*

It's one man's car, and a beautiful one at that — a 1937 Packard One Twenty convertible coupe, owned by Page Gilman, who played Jack Barbour on the long-popular network radio program, "One Man's Family."

Standing beside his new 1937 Packard Super Eight victoria is Yurek Shabelevsky, star of the Col. W. deBasil Ballets Russe. He purchased the car from a Packard dealer in Detroit.

Comedian Jack Benny did not always drive a Maxwell. Rumor persists that, to pay for this beautiful 1937 Packard Twelve formal sedan, he had to transfer a wheelbarrow-load of coins from the vault in his basement. One of America's greatest entertainers, Benny was a star of radio, television, the movies and the stage.

Early in 1937, Henry Cabot Lodge, Jr. (right), U.S. senator from Massachusetts, and Mrs. Lodge took delivery of this Packard convertible sedan from John A. Trowt, representing the Packard dealer in Beverly Farms. Lodge was Richard M. Nixon's running mate for vice-president in the 1960 national election.

Proof that Powel Crosley, despite his above-average height, preferred smaller cars even before he began building them himself, is demonstrated by this picture. The president of the Crosley Radio Corporation, of radio station WLW and the Cincinnati Reds baseball team (the tallest in the group of five behind the car) came to Toledo to take delivery of the 50,000th Willys car off the assembly line, a 1937 model. In all, 63,467 Willys models were manufactured that year, all smaller than conventional U.S. cars. The Crosley car, produced between 1939 and 1952, was one of the smallest American cars ever built, and modestly successful for its time.

Baseball great Babe Ruth appears again, this time with a 1937 Nash Ambassador Eight sedan, built in the year of the merger of Nash Motors Company and Kelvinator Corporation to form Nash-Kelvinator. While most baseball fans know of Ruth's prowess as a baseball slugger, many are unaware of his success as a pitcher in his early days. During World War I, for example, he pitched twenty-nine and two-thirds consecutive innings without allowing an earned run, a record.

Al Schacht, the baseball player who turned to pantomimic buffoonery, is shown with his 1937 Packard One Twenty convertible coupe. Schacht pitched for the Washington Senators from 1919 to 1921, then joined Nick Altrock in entertaining baseball crowds throughout the American League for a number of years in pre-game shows.

Waving from an open Packard to a welcoming crowd in Milwaukee is Douglas "Wrong Way" Corrigan, the aviator who startled the world on July 17, 1938 when he flew nonstop from New York to Ireland in an ancient Curtiss Robin J-6 monoplane that he thought was headed west to California. Just the day before he had landed at Floyd Bennett Airfield after setting a nonstop transcontinental record of less than twenty-eight hours. He flew across the Atlantic most of the way through dense fog, with no radio or compass.

Irving "Bump" Hadley, then a pitcher for the New York Yankees baseball team, bought this 1938 Packard Eight sedan from a Packard dealer in the Bronx. Hadley began his major league career with the Washington Senators in 1926.

Seated in his 1938 Lincoln Zephyr convertible coupe is Mickey Cochrane, famed American League catcher who was inducted into the National Baseball Hall of Fame in 1947. Cochrane played with the Philadelphia Athletics from 1925 to 1934, when he was traded to the Detroit Tigers, who made him a playing manager. He played and managed to 1937.

A unique brand of hillbilly humor led Bob Burns, pictured with his elegant 1938 Packard Eight convertible coupe, to fame. Born in Van Buren, Arkansas, he developed a successful vaudeville and nightclub act involving comedy and a crude wind instrument he invented and called a bazooka. He carried his success to films and radio. Burns was at the height of his career in 1938, when he appeared in three films — **The Arkansas Traveler,** **Tropic Holiday** and **Radio City Revels.**

Photographed with a 1938 Buick Special convertible are Hollywood stars Jackie Coogan and Betty Grable, who were married at the time and appearing together in the film **College Swing.** Coogan was born in Los Angeles in 1914. His first motion picture was **Sinner's Baby** at the age of eighteen months. Charlie Chaplin used him at four in the two-reeler, **A Day's Pleasure,** in 1919. Two years later, Coogan was co-starring with Chaplin in the famed feature-length film **The Kid.** Coogan went on to become one of the most successful child stars in film history. Betty Grable, whom he married in 1937, was born in St. Louis in 1916. She worked for various studios, appearing in musicals and period pictures, including **Moon Over Miami** in 1941, **Sweet Rosie O'Grady** in 1943 and **Mother Wore Tights** in 1947. She divorced Coogan in 1939 and married band leader Harry James in 1943.

Tennis champions Donald Budge (left) and C. Gene Mako while on tour in Australia in 1938 drove out to see Sydney Harbor and the bridge in their Packard touring sedan. Budge and Mako were U.S. Tennis Association doubles champions in 1936 and 1938.

Ted Weems (left), the popular orchestra leader, is pictured with a new car again — this time a 1938 Hudson Eight sedan.

Charles W. Nash had earned a well-deserved retirement in California when this picture of him was taken with his 1938 Nash cabriolet. While retaining the title of chairman of the board of Nash-Kelvinator Corporation, created a year earlier when Nash Motors Company merged with Kelvinator Corporation, he left the decision-making to George W. Mason, president. One of the great pioneers in the auto industry, Nash had an orphaned childhood, and with little formal education became president of Buick, then president of General Motors from which he resigned in 1916 to start a company under his own name.

During their tour of the United States and Canada in 1939, Great Britain's King George VI and Queen Elizabeth frequently rode in this Lincoln V-12 convertible sedan which was built especially for their use. The custom LeBaron body incorporated shatterproof glass surrounding the rear compartment, extra-high seats and richly-appointed interior. The car, used again in 1957 by Queen Elizabeth II and Prince Philip on their visit to North America, is on exhibit at the Henry Ford Museum in Dearborn, Michigan. This picture was taken in Regina, Saskatchewan, Canada.

An official visit to the White House was a highlight of their tour of North America by the royal couple. A beaming President Franklin D. Roosevelt rides with King George VI in the back seat of a 1939 Packard Twelve convertible sedan.

One of the most historic addresses ever made by Winston Churchill was given at Westminster College in Fulton, Missouri in 1946. Invited to appear there by President Harry Truman, Churchill gave his famous "Iron Curtain" speech. In a parade through the small Missouri town, the two world leaders are standing in the rear of the much-photographed 1939 Lincoln convertible sedan known as the "Sunshine Special," the official White House car used by Presidents Franklin D. Roosevelt and Truman. After it was retired from service in 1950, it was donated to the Henry Ford Museum in Dearborn, Michigan.

It was the first model year for the Mercury, Ford Motor Company's entrant in the medium-priced field, and one of the first to get one was Lowell Thomas, the radio news-caster, shown here with a 1939 convertible coupe.

A salesman (left) gives the keys to a 1939 Pontiac to the comedian W. C. Fields, outside the stage entrance to a film studio in Hollywood. While many moviegoers remember Fields for his hilarious roles in films (such as **So's Your Old Man** in 1926 and **My Little Chickadee** in 1940 with Mae West), probably his most memorable performance was a serious one — as Micawber in the 1935 epic **David Copperfield.**

199

Judy Garland was seventeen years old when this photo was taken of her with a 1939 Packard Six. Already she was a world-famous star for her marvelous performance in **The Wizard of Oz.** Born Frances Gumm in Grand Rapids, Minnesota, of vaudeville parents, she made her stage debut at three and was a seasoned trouper at five. When she was nine, her name was changed to Judy Garland at the suggestion of George Jessel. Her first big hit was **Broadway Melody of 1938,** when she sang "Dear Mr. Gable" to the Hollywood star's photograph. She co-starred with Mickey Rooney nine times, beginning with **Thoroughbreds Don't Cry** in 1937.

Gene Autry, the "Singing Cowboy" who starred in ninety-five feature films, told an interviewer in March 1982: "In all those pictures I never took a drink, never shot an Indian, never carried a girl off to the bedroom and never punched anyone smaller than me." He is pictured (left) with a 1939 Chevrolet sedan. Autry also starred in 100 television shows and made many successful recordings. More than 100 million copies of his "Rudolph the Red-nosed Reindeer" have been sold. He owns the California Angels baseball team in the American League. (The author remembers following him around Flint, Michigan during World War II as the famous cowboy star then in an Army uniform urged young women to join the Women's Army Corps.)

Golfer Byron Nelson (left), with Mrs. Nelson, takes delivery of a 1939 sedan from the president of Willys-Overland, Joseph W. Frazer, who a few years later was to join Henry J. Kaiser in forming Kaiser-Frazer Corporation. The picture was taken at Toledo's Inverness course where Nelson, National Open champion, had just signed a contract to become club professional. He went on to win the PGA twice and the Masters twice. A note about the car: While the name Willys-Overland appears on the hood, the company later decided to call all 1939 models by the Overland name.

In the fall of 1940, during his campaign for an unprecedented third term, President Franklin D. Roosevelt visited the submarine base at New London, Connecticut where the 1,750-ton U.S.S. Tautog, largest type submarine called for under the new defense program, was being built. With the President in the 1939 Packard Twelve convertible sedan are Capt. H. M. Jensen, base commandant, and Connecticut's Senator Francis T. Maloney and Governor Raymond E. Baldwin.

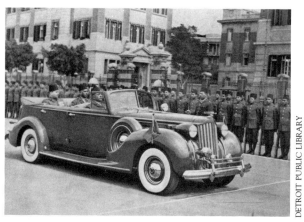

King Farouk I of Egypt, riding in the royal 1939 Packard Twelve convertible sedan, inspects his troops. The car is one of a fleet of eleven Packards which included a special armored sedan.

Doff Aber, well known in the West as a champion bronco rider, owned this 1939 Pontiac eight-cylinder coupe.

New York's popular mayor, Fiorello LaGuardia (back seat, right), rode in a rare Packard on the occasion of the dedication of a link in the East River Drive on June 25, 1940. With him are Stanley Isaacs, Manhattan borough president, and Mrs. Isaacs, and the link was from 49th to 92nd Streets. The handsome car is a 1940 Packard One Eighty convertible sedan, with body by Darrin. Only ten were made.

202

John R. Cobb, holder of the world's automobile record at the time (368.85 miles per hour), stands between his Railton Red Lion racer and a 1940 Hudson Eight stock sedan, which he drove to a record ninety-three and nine-tenths miles per hour on the Bonneville Salt Flats in Utah, in August 1939.

Veteran actor Walter Pidgeon, seen earlier with a 1930 Cadillac, is pictured here with a 1940 Plymouth station wagon which appeared in the film **The House Across the Bay** in which he starred. In that period, station wagons were specialty vehicles with wooden panels that had to be virtually custom-built.

General Dwight D. Eisenhower waves from a 1940 Chrysler Crown Imperial phaeton in the New York City parade that celebrated the end of World War II. The traditional ticker-tape parade was held on June 19, 1945. Few motorcars have been seen by more millions of people than this phaeton with its hand-made custom body by Derham. Now on exhibit at the Henry Ford Museum in Dearborn, Michigan, it was used by the City of New York as its official parade car for more than twenty years before its retirement in 1960.

As an independent industrial designer, George W. Walker was engaged by Nash Motors to style its new cars for 1940. Walker told the author years later that in creating the distinctive Nash grille, he was influenced by the front-end design of the LaSalle, built by General Motors.

COMMENTARY

Nash-Kelvinator's modest public relations staff early in June 1948 was located on the east side of the third floor of the company's administration building on Plymouth Road in Detroit. The executive offices were within running distance on the west side.

This positioning is important in understanding how some of the public relations people could hear the verbal explosion that emanated from the office of George W. Mason, chairman and president, when for the first time he saw pictures of the all-new 1949 Ford car.

The public relations director, Fred L. Black, who rushed down to Mason's office, told us later he heard Mason swear, as only he could, that "George Walker has given the goddam Nash design to Ford." What Mason referred to was a new model design that Walker's independent industrial design studio had created during the latter war years for Nash Motors' first new postwar car. We did not know it then, but Mason was planning a small short-wheelbase car for introduction early in 1950, and the Walker design was going to be used.

Black told us a few hours later that Mason had called Walker to demand to know why the Nash design went to Ford. Walker's rather meek reply was to the effect that Nash had the prototype design for more than five years, and he assumed it was not going to be used.

In a telephone conversation I had with Walker in Tucson, Arizona, in 1979, he confirmed the facts concerning the call he received from George Mason. "Hell, I figured Nash wasn't going to use the design. It was a good one, so I had it modified a little and it became the 1949 Ford," Walker told me.

Walker, of course, became an instant hero at Ford after the new Ford came out. Sales in 1949 almost doubled the 1948 total, and Ford Motor Company was restored to profitability.

Meanwhile, back at Nash Motors, Mason ordered the engineering staff to change the front-end design of what became the Nash Rambler, introduced in March 1950.

As things developed, Nash did all right with its new design, too, although it was not as immediate a success. The Rambler concept eventually produced unprecedented production, sales and earnings for the company, following the merger with Hudson in 1954 to create American Motors Corporation.

A happy owner of a 1940 Packard One Eighty convertible victoria with a custom body by Darrin was Gene Krupa, then playing at the Sherman Hotel in Chicago. America's ace drummer and orchestra leader had his car finished in Packard cream with red wheels.

Taking delivery of a 1940 Packard is the famous wrestler, Maurice Tillet, better known as "The Angel."

John Archer, his face in shadow, is behind the wheel of this 1940 Pontiac Deluxe Eight cabriolet. An RKO actor, Archer entered films in 1938 after winning a talent contest. He played leads in B pictures and supporting roles in A productions. When this picture was taken, he was filming **Curtain Call**.

Henry "Hot Lips" Busse, the famed orchestra leader, and Mrs. Busse took delivery at the factory of this 1940 Packard Super Eight 160 convertible coupe.

Eddie Cantor shows off the new front end of the 1940 Nash. Cantor was a household word in America for a generation. He started out in vaudeville, starred on Broadway and in the movies and became an instant hit on network radio. He was sponsored for years by Chase & Sanborn coffee which one of his cast of characters referred to as "Chafed and Sunburn."

During the torrid campaign for the presidency in 1940, Wendell Wilkie from Indiana unsuccessfully challenged Franklin D. Roosevelt, who was running for an uprecedented third term. The Republican candidate is shown here waving to an Iowa crowd from a 1940 Packard Super Eight Convertible sedan.

Judy Garland appears again, this time with the 1940 Studebaker Champion she owned while in Hollywood. The world-famous star was married five times. Her second marriage, to Vincent Minnelli in 1944, followed the successful film **Meet Me in St. Louis.** Their daughter, Liza Minnelli, born in 1946, is now a famous entertainer in her own right. Judy Garland gave many memorable concerts in London and the United States in the final years before her death in 1969.

Former heavyweight champion Max Baer gives some pointers to his son, a willing learner, in front of a 1940 Chrysler New Yorker convertible. Baer was champion in 1934 and 1935.

Ed "Porky" Oliver, the professional golfer, sits behind the wheel of his new 1940 Packard One Ten convertible coupe.

Anna Kaskas, Metropolitan Opera star, came home to Hartford, Connecticut to take delivery of her new 1940 Packard touring sedan from L. G. Burnham, salesman for Packard's Hartford branch.

The great Hollywood actor Spencer Tracy appears with two automobiles of the early 1940s. The top photo shows him with a 1940 Lincoln Zephyr club coupe. Taken at Greenfield Village in Dearborn, Michigan, it shows Henry Ford in the back seat and Edsel Ford behind the wheel. Tracy was visiting the Thomas A. Edison laboratories which Henry Ford had moved there from Menlo Park. The occasion was the filming of **Edison the Man.** *In the bottom photo Tracy stands beside a 1941 Chevrolet station wagon which he was awarded for being named "ranking favorite among all movie stars" by readers of* **Friends,** *the Chevrolet owner magazine. W. G. Lewellen, Chevrolet sales executive, makes the presentation. An alltime film favorite, Spencer Tracy made many memorable pictures, including* **Twenty Thousand Years in Sing Sing** *in 1932,* **San Francisco** *in 1936,* **Captains Courageous** *(for which he won an Oscar) in 1937,* **Father of the Bride** *in 1940 and* **Inherit the Wind** *in 1960.*

The Irish tennis champion, George Lyttleton-Rogers, explains to two friends why he bought a 1941 Packard Clipper sedan. At six feet eight inches, he towers over them. Lyttleton-Rogers played in Davis Cup competition for twelve consecutive years.

Modeling a new two-toned gown designed by Vera West, fashion designer for Universal Pictures, is actress Peggy Moran, who had just completed **Flying Cadets** for Universal. Also in the photo is a two-toned 1941 Nash '600,' so named because it offered a maximum of thirty miles per gallon of gasoline on a twenty-gallon tank. When Nash Motors introduced this car with unitized construction in the fall of 1940, it was an immediate success in the low-priced field.

Waving from the back seat of a 1941 Packard 160 convertible sedan is General Jonathan Wainwright, only three weeks out of a Japanese prison camp in the Philippines. The occasion is a homecoming parade in Skaneateles, New York in September 1945. The distinctive car, then owned by Henry Dutton Noble of Auburn, New York, at this writing belongs to Robert Mehl of Grand Island, New York.

209

The president of Hudson Motor Car Company, A. E. Barit, shown here with a 1941 Hudson Commodore custom sedan, liked to wear white linen suits in the summer. He succeeded Roy D. Chapin in 1936 as chief executive of the Hudson Motor Car Company and helped negotiate the merger with Nash-Kelvinator Corporation in 1954 to create American Motors.

The man after whom the Oldsmobile was named, automotive pioneer Ransom E. Olds, smiles from behind the wheel of a 1941 convertible model. In a dispute over product policies, Olds left Oldsmobile in 1904 to form his own Reo Motor Car Company. Oldsmobile became part of General Motors in 1909.

This unusual photo was taken at Ledara Heights in Southern California when the tract was opened in 1941. The car is a 1941 Pontiac sedan, and the young woman is actress Evelyn Keyes, who played Scarlett O'Hara's sister in **Gone With The Wind** and appeared in many movies for Columbia in the 1940s. She was filming **Here Comes Mr. Jordan** when this picture was taken.

In this series of four photographs, the bulwark vehicle of the armed services, the military Jeep, carries important dignitaries during World War II. The unique four-wheel-drive Jeep, developed originally as a reconnaissance vehicle, was produced during the war by Willys-Overland in Toledo, Ohio, and by Ford Motor Company in Dearborn, Michigan. More than 585,000 saw service on all war fronts and at bases in the U.S. and Europe. After the war, Willys registered the Jeep trademark and brought out civilian versions of the famous quarter-ton vehicle. Jeep vehicles in a wide variety of configurations today are produced in Toledo by a subsidiary of American Motors Corporation. Jeeps also are produced in many other countries of the world.

President Franklin D. Roosevelt salutes the American flag during a surprise trip to North Africa early in the war.

Again riding in a military Jeep, the President reviews the troops.

Somewhere in the Southwest Pacific, General Douglas MacArthur sits somberly in a Jeep. Of the seven men pictured, only one is smiling.

Sitting next to the soldier driving a Jeep is General Mark Clark, leading a group of Americans into Paris as the direction of the war finally turns toward victory for the Allies.

President Franklin D. Roosevelt sits in a military Jeep to be photographed for posterity at the 1945 Yalta Conference with Joseph Stalin and Winston Churchill. Stalin, however, is said to have refused to appear in this picture, so the Soviet Union is represented by Vyacheslav Molotov, at Churchill's right. Note how drawn Roosevelt's face appears.

1946-1982: *Subject to Change*

Once the unprecedented demand for new cars in the United States was met following four war years of unavailability, intense competition returned to the automobile market. Trends that had begun earlier became more pronounced, and while production totals and profits each year established new records for the major companies, it was apparent the industry was avoiding impending problems. It also was apparent that dramatic change was coming.

The industry each year rushed to bring out longer, wider, heavier and more powerful automobiles — in the face of parking spaces that remained the same size, of streets and roads that were not getting wider or longer, of alarming increases in traffic accidents and fatalities.

Legislation passed during the Eisenhower administration eventually brought a network of interstate freeways and vastly-improved state roads. Cars, however, continued to get bigger, and Americans in increasing numbers began to look at imported cars which were smaller and less expensive. It was only a mild trend, of course, until the energy shortage of the mid-1970's struck America and the rest of the world like a thunderbolt. Not only did sales of foreign cars leap to a record share of the total market, but the U.S. manufacturers almost overnight had to meet rigid Government standards that could be met only by building much smaller cars powered by much smaller engines.

Along the way, the industry had to contend with several economic recessions, wars in Korea and Vietnam, worldwide inflation and high interest rates. Despite the many hurdles, however, the U.S auto industry managed in the postwar period through most of 1982 to produce nearly 250 million passenger cars, close to four times as many as were built before the war. Whether such levels can continue to the end of this century and beyond is unknown, of course, but the average American who dearly loves his or her car can take comfort in the fact that while the U.S.-built automobile of today is much smaller, it still offers the luxury and performance of the traditional big American car of the past. But it now has advantages not generally available before. It costs far less to operate and maintain. It is easier to park and maneuver in traffic. It is built better.

*   *   *   *   *   *

As the reader can see, the parade of cars with personalities as it passes into the postwar period is getting noticeably thinner. Several reasons account for this. First is the growing lack of interest on the part of newspaper and magazine editors in publishing pictures of prominent people with cars. Second, if an editor does show an interest, he or she probably would rather arrange to have the publication take its own pictures — and too often the personality so dominates the photo that the car is scarcely visible. Third, some prominent figures have sharp agents who will not agree to let their clients be photographed with cars unless a handsome fee is paid. But perhaps the most important reason is simply that the automobile has lost its appeal as a status symbol. Now it is not so much what *kind* of car a personality owns — but how *many*.

It was a sight to behold — Kaiser and Frazer automobile bodies coming down a line more than a mile long, in little more than a year after war's end. The Liberator bomber plant operated by Ford Motor Company at Willow Run west of Detroit was converted into a modern automobile assembly plant by the new Kaiser-Frazer Corporation, anxious to get its share of the booming postwar market for new cars.

The driver of this classic 1946 Lincoln Continental cabriolet is Ronald Reagan, when he was a prominent motion picture actor. Thomas F. Lerch, of North Canton, Ohio, sent a copy of the Continental Owners Club publication with this photograph on the cover to President Reagan in 1981. His secretary advised that the president could not recall the identity of the woman riding with him in the picture but that he remembered she was a Swedish actress. During his Hollywood career, Reagan appeared in about fifty films, mostly of the B variety. He starred in **Hell's Kitchen** in 1939, **Knute Rockne All-American** in 1940 and **Kings Row** in 1942. He married Jane Wyman in 1940. They were divorced in 1948. He married Nancy Davis in 1952. For three years Reagan was host of "Death Valley Days" on TV, then for eight years on the "General Electric Theater." He starred in many of the program's dramatic episodes.

Hank Greenberg, star first baseman for the Detroit Tigers, is pictured with a 1946 Lincoln sedan, one of the first to be produced following World War II. Greenberg, who had a lifetime batting average of .313, will be remembered as one of several sluggers who "almost" equaled Babe Ruth's magical sixty home runs in a single year. Hank hammered out fifty-eight in 1938. He was elected to the National Baseball Hall of Fame in 1956.

"The Body" in this instance does not refer to the beautiful wood-grain side panels on this 1946 Chrysler Town and Country convertible, but to Marie McDonald standing beside it. That was what film publicists called the young actress, born Marie Frye in 1923. Her first picture was **It Started with Eve** in 1941. Others were **Tell it to the Judge** in 1949 and **Once a Thief** in 1950. She was married seven times.

One of the first Packards built after World War II went to five-star General Henry Harley "Hap" Arnold, shown with his DeLuxe Clipper sedan. He was chief of the Army Air Forces during the war and was named general of the army in 1944.

Inventor William B. Stout stands beside his revolutionary rear-engine Scarab car. The photograph was taken in 1946 at Toledo, where Stout was trying to persuade Willys-Overland to put his car into production. Earlier, in 1935 and 1936, a few Scarab models of a different design were hand-built, but volume production was never achieved.

COMMENTARY

I first met Bill Stout during the Automotive Golden Jubilee in Detroit when he joined industry pioneers and dignitaries on the reviewing stand for the huge parade. I'll never forget that June 1, not only because in my role as personal aide to Charles Brady King I stood on that reviewing stand, but also because it was a bitter cold day. With thousands of people packed in all directions from the stand, located on Woodward Avenue near Detroit's old city hall, it was not long before Bill Stout, who had a pixyish sense of humor, began asking how many others, besides himself, needed to go to the bathroom. Of course, in the cold after several hours, that can become a problem. Stout continued hammering on the theme, however, *forcing* us to think about it. Finally, it was too much for Charles W. Nash and King, both of whom demanded to know what provisions had been made for such an emergency. I was delegated by George Romney, Jubilee chairman then general manager of the Automobile Manufacturers Association, to take both of them through the mass of humanity to the basement of the city hall. It was not as commanding a task as I had feared because others in the crowd had the same idea, and many led the way.

Many times I sat with Bill Stout and one of his best friends, Fred L. Black, my boss at Nash-Kelvinator, at luncheon meetings of the Adcraft Club of Detroit, held then in the Statler Hotel. Stout told many tales of his experiences in the early days of the auto industry, particularly about his involvement in the design of the Imp cyclecar.

One of the last times I saw him was when he invited several of us who had been guests of Fred and Ruth Black at the Orchard Lake Country Club to come to his home not far away. He showed us the latest model of his revolutionary Scarab car and took us in small groups for rides around the grounds. He engaged in a constant running account of how different the sleek-looking Scarab was from all other cars — almost as though he were giving the same pitch that he had used unsuccessfully with so many investors and producers, hoping to get them to help put the car into production. I remember one unusual feature — upholstered chairs, not fixed to the floor, that could be moved about with ease. Safety considerations apparently had little bearing on ideas in those days.

As the aide to Charles B. King during the Automotive Golden Jubilee in Detroit in 1946, I sat at one of the tables closest to the speakers' dais during the pioneers' tribute dinner at the Masonic Temple. At the same table were, among other dignitaries, Lowell Thomas, the newscaster, and William B. Stout. When Stout found out I was with Nash-Kelvinator, he quickly penciled on the back of my program this sketch of a Nash car with Kelvinator refrigeration.

Almost as soon as World War II ended, a new competitor in the automobile industry, Kaiser-Frazer Corporation, began laying plans to produce passenger cars in the giant plant at Willow Run, near Detroit, where Ford Motor Company had built Liberator bombers during the war. Henry J. Kaiser, who had amassed a fortune in steel and aluminum, joined forces with Joseph W. Frazer, a seasoned auto executive who had been president of both Willys-Overland and Graham-Paige. They built Kaiser and Frazer sedans at first. Eva Marie Saint, then a Broadway star, sits on the hood of a 1947 Frazer Manhattan. Seven years later she won an Oscar for her first film, **On the Waterfront.**

The pent-up demand for new cars immediately after World War II was so intense that almost any car that could be produced in the face of shortages of steel, rubber, aluminum and other critical materials was snapped up immediately. And almost anyone could sell new cars, including Shep Fields, the popular orchestra leader, shown with his wife beside a 1947 Frazer, photographed at the Kaiser-Frazer plant at Willow Run. He has just signed a contract to be the company's dealer in a new facility at New Rochelle, New York.

CADILLAC MOTOR CAR DIVISION

Roy Rogers, one of Hollywood's most popular singing cowboys, takes on a 1947 Cadillac. He changed his name twice. Born Leonard Slye in Cincinnati in 1912, he changed his name in the mid-1930s to Dick Weston and formed a singing group called the "Sons of the Pioneers" which appeared on Los Angeles radio and in films. Later he became Roy Rogers, starring in many lively Westerns through the early 1950s with his wife (since 1947), Dale Evans, and his famous horse Trigger.

Rita Hayworth, beautiful actress who starred in thirty-nine motion pictures from 1937 to 1967, poses with a 1947 Lincoln. Among her most-remembered films are **Angels Over Broadway** in 1940, **Gilda** in 1946, **Affair in Trinidad** in 1952, **Miss Sadie Thompson** in 1953 and **Pal Joey** in 1957.

Here is film star Clark Gable again, this time about to enter a Lincoln Continental cabriolet, built early in 1947. The classic Continental, designed under the direction of Edsel Ford, was built in limited numbers from 1940 to 1948.

Even baseball players were excited about the 1947 Frazer. This photograph, released by Kaiser-Frazer August 15, 1946, carried this caption: "There's no doubt of the 'fielders' choice' as Connie Mack and his charges, leaving their Washington hotel for yesterday's twin bill with the Senators, examine the first Frazer to arrive in the Capital. Left to right are: Oscar Grimes, Louis Knerr, Mrs. Barney McCoskey, McCoskey, Mack, Lum Harriss, Trainer Jim Tradley, Coach Dave Keep and Sam Chapman." Mack, associated with the Philadelphia Athletics for fifty-three years as player, manager and club owner, died in 1956 at ninety-three.

President Harry Truman stands beside an official White House car just delivered, a 1947 Cadillac Series Seventy-Five Fleetwood limousine.

Bing Crosby, whose crooning voice and relaxed humor entertained millions around the world for half a century, sits on the bumper of a 1947 Cadillac with Robert O. Reynolds (left), Cadillac sales executive. Crosby was one of the most popular singers of all time, selling tens of millions of records. He was a favorite throughout the world in motion pictures, on radio and on television. He died at seventy-three in 1977 after a round of golf in Madrid, Spain.

When a canary yellow Nash Ambassador sedan was selected to pace the Indianapolis 500 on Memorial Day 1947, motion picture idol Clark Gable asked if he could take the car for a spin. George W. Mason (right), president of Nash-Kelvinator Corporation who later drove the car to pace the race, not only agreed but also suggested they have their picture taken together afterward.

Almost obscuring the beautiful 1948 Packard sedan behind them are the orchestra leader Spike Jones and his girl singer Dorothy Shay. The photograph was taken in front of the Statler Hotel in Detroit. Probably no one in show business had more fun than Spike Jones, who gathered together a group of musicians who could play home-made instruments made of tin cans, washboards and other unlikely items.

Arthur Godfrey, for many years one of the most popular radio personalities and who later starred on television with his "Talent Scouts" program, waves from a 1948 Studebaker Commander convertible in a welcoming parade. Studebaker was the first with an all-new postwar car, of the companies that were building automobiles prior to the war. The new Studebakers, designed by Raymond Loewy, were introduced in mid-1946.

Art Linkletter, longtime star of radio and television, is driving this 1948 Studebaker Champion convertible. For years he was host of the popular "House Party" programs and was noted for his uncanny ability to get children to express themselves without coaching.

As World War II ended, many small companies announced plans to build cars to meet a huge pent-up demand. One of the most interesting was a firm in Buffalo, New York that hoped to market a car called the Playboy. Here are two models photographed on the grounds of the Ambassador Hotel in Los Angeles in 1948. The car at left has the top up in conventional coupe fashion, while the other has the steel top lowered, making it a convertible. Standing are Robert McKenzie (left), engineer of the Playboy Motor Car Corporation, and Ben G. Kohn, president of Inter-Trade Associates, Ltd., of New York, worldwide agency for the car. From 1946 to 1951, only 97 Playboys were produced.

The noted ballad singer and actor Burl Ives demonstrates the convenience features of the new 1949 Kaiser Traveler. Its unique tailgate doors which permitted cargo to be loaded and unloaded from the back marked the Traveler as the forerunner of the present-day hatchback models. Born in 1909 as Burl Ide Ivanhoe, Burl Ives with his paunchy figure, beard and ready smile, played both villains and heroes in Hollywood films and on television.

Twenty years after being shown in a 1929 Packard, figure skating star Sonja Henie appears in a beautiful 1949 Cadillac convertible. With her is Donald Ahrens, Cadillac general manager. The photograph was taken in late 1948.

CADILLAC MOTOR CAR DIVISION

OLDSMOBILE DIVISION

Veteran race driver-Wilbur Shaw drove this 1949 Oldsmobile convertible as the pace car in the Indianapolis 500 classic on Memorial Day 1949.

Driving the official pace car, a Mercury convertible, at the Indianapolis 500-mile race on May 30, 1950, is Benson Ford, one of three sons of Edsel Ford.

INDIANAPOLIS MOTOR SPEEDWAY

After World War II, a number of small companies began building automobiles for selected markets. Shown is a 1950 Kurtis sports car, designed and built by Frank Kurtis (right). Kurtis-Kraft, Inc. turned out sixty-two of these handsome convertibles in 1949 and 1950. In December 1954, the company was reorganized as Kurtis Sports Car Corporation, offering another sports model known as the Kurtis 500-M. Kurtis here shows the early version to W. L. Rodgers.

*Robert Z. Leonard, veteran film director, posed on a Hollywood lot with his new 1950 Packard Custom Eight sedan. The metal sun visor was a popular accessory available on almost all U.S.-built cars that year. Among Leonard's many successful films were **The Bachelor Father** in 1930, **The Great Ziegfeld** in 1936 and **Girl of the Golden West** in 1938.*

President Dwight D. Eisenhower, who almost always waved both hands to crowds, was photographed October 17, 1960 during a visit to Detroit. He is riding in the 1950 Lincoln convertible limousine, designed for presidential parades and special state functions. It was used by four presidents, from Truman to Johnson. Since its retirement in 1967, it has been on exhibit at the Henry Ford Museum in Dearborn, Michigan.

*Hollywood star Jane Wyman is pictured in a 1950 Mercury convertible in the driveway of her home. Born in St. Joseph, Missouri in 1914 as Sarah Jane Fulks, she began her career as a radio vocalist. She appeared in several film musicals as a chorus dancer before her first picture as an actress, **Gold Diggers of 1937.** She won an Academy Award as best actress for **Johnny Belinda** in 1948, the year she divorced Ronald Reagan after nearly nine years of marriage. Miss Wyman later starred on several television shows.*

George W. Mason, president of Nash-Kelvinator Corporation, sits behind the wheel of the unique experimental car that Nash Motors showed to selected audiences across the United States early in 1950, to measure public interest. Called the N.X.I. (for Nash Experimental International), it was the prototype of what became the little Nash Metropolitan, built in England by Austin and sold primarily in the U.S. and Canada from 1954 to 1962.

The N.X.I. was a carefully-planned market study car, conceived by Mason and communicated to the press and key opinion makers in 1950 by George Romney (right), vice-president of Nash-Kelvinator. Romney here details the car's features to the famed Italian coachbuilder Pinin Farina (nearest camera) and his son-in-law Renzo Carli (at the wheel), as Ted Ulrich, Nash body engineer, looks on.

COMMENTARY

How the N.X.I. came to be is one of the most unusual stories of the postwar automobile industry.

It began in 1948, when George W. Mason, president of Nash-Kelvinator Corporation, and Meade F. Moore, Nash vice-president of engineering and research, decided to explore the possibility of building a little two-seater car. Mason approached William Flajole, an independent Detroit designer, and asked him to submit sketches of a car he had in mind. The entire project was cloaked in secrecy of an order much higher than was usual in the auto industry at that time.

Flajole was told that the front wheels of the model were to be enclosed (a Nash trademark then), and that it would be a unitized construction car. Flajole and his staff came up with a number of sketches, and Mason selected one that is quite similar to the eventual prototype. It was called "Fiat Traveler," so outsiders would not identify it with Nash.

With the initial sketch approved, Flajole, working with Nash engineers, built a complete convertible model. Finished in a deep maroon, it was powered by a small four-cylinder Fiat engine of eighteen horsepower. It was given the name Nash Experimental International (N.X.I.).

Late in 1949, Mason made a decision for which he has not been given full credit. Instead of electing to produce the car, he chose to go to the American public and ask potential car buyers if the N.X.I. concept was appealing enough to warrant putting the car into production. Never before in U.S. auto history had an automobile been shown to the public before the decision had been made to build it.

Enter George Romney. In January 1950, he was a Nash-Kelvinator vice-president who shared Mason's fervor for the small car and saw a rare opportunity to attract broad national attention to the company's engineering and research capability. Mason chose him to direct a series of by-invitation-only showings of the N.X.I. in key U.S. cities.

Highlight of the triumphant tour of the little car was its appearance at the Waldorf-Astoria in New York. Ranking members of the business and financial community showed up to inspect the N.X.I., and a number of executives of the other companies, by invitation, made appearances. I was deeply involved in much of the preparation for this showing and all others except those held on the West Coast. My job was to obtain lists of guests, to handle the printing and mailing of invitations and advise all concerned of the daily responses.

The showings were called "surviews" — for survey-preview — since not only was the objective to show the car to influential people, but also to circulate more than 250,000 questionnaires, which posed the question "Does America Want the Economy Car?"

So as not to lock itself in, Nash Motors also showed at each surview two other, more powerful engines which could be used if the national survey showed the eighteen-horsepower Fiat engine was too small. The two engines, attractively mounted on stands, were a thirty-six horsepower Fiat and a thirty-six horsepower British Standard.

The N.X.I. was unique in many ways. Its front grille and bumper were combined into a single unit, with the same design carried out in the rear bumper unit, except that the spare tire was housed in the grille opening. The hood, front fenders and lights were combined in one assembly which could be raised for easy servicing.

Three months later the company announced that the national survey showed a "widespread general interest in a small, quality, high-style car." Among the thousands of suggestions, blueprints and drawings which came with the returned questionnaires, greatest emphasis was placed on the following: Instead of the divided front seat in the prototype, respondents favored a single seat, proving room for three instead of two passengers. Definite preference was expressed for the thirty-six horsepower engine.

By the time the 1951 auto shows were held, Mason reported that the N.X.I. was still under development, and that the name had been changed to N.K.I. (for Nash-Kelvinator International). He said that Nash engineers had built three prototypes — a convertible, a hardtop convertible and a standard coupe. Each had a wheelbase of eighty-five inches and was powered by a European engine which gave thirty-five to forty miles to the gallon of gasoline.

On October 5, 1952, Mason announced that negotiations had been completed with two British firms to begin production during the latter part of 1953 of a new small car for distribution in the U.S. and Canada. He said Fisher & Ludlow, Ltd. would build the bodies, and Austin Motor Company, Ltd. would provide the engine and chassis and do the final assembly. The car, christened the Nash Metropolitan, was placed on sale in North America in March 1954. After the merger of Nash-Kelvinator and Hudson in May of that year, and for the next two model years, the car was either a Nash or a Hudson Metropolitan, depending on which dealer sold it. From 1957 through 1962, it became a name on its own.

Talk about a posed publicity picture. Arriving from Honolulu, Eddie Peabody (left), the famous banjo king, takes delivery of his new 1950 Cadillac Sixty-Two coupe at the airport in Sioux Falls, South Dakota. There to complete the sale is Frank A. Prather, the local Cadillac distributor.

The Duke and Duchess of Windsor bought this 1950 Buick Super Model 59 estate wagon.

CADILLAC MOTOR CAR DIVISION

Behind the wheel of a 1951 Cadillac convertible is actress Jan Sterling. She was filming **Appointment With Danger** at the time. She was nominated for an Oscar in 1954 for her excellent performance in **The High and the Mighty.** Miss Sterling, married to Paul Douglas, also appeared in **Slaughter on Tenth Avenue** in 1957. She returned in 1976 to the screen after a long absence.

As photographs appearing earlier in this book can attest, E. G. "Cannon Ball" Baker was engaged by most of the major auto companies to prove the performance claims of their products. At the Willow Run offices of Kaiser-Frazer Corporation, Baker poses with a 1951 Kaiser sedan with which he established endurance and speed records.

Posing with a 1951 Henry J sedan are Shaye Cogan and James Alexander, stars of the film **Jack and the Beanstalk** which was released in 1952. The Henry J was Kaiser-Frazer Corporation's entry into the low-priced field. A smaller car than the Kaiser and the Frazer, the Willow Run product lasted through the 1954 year.

An unusual 1951 Kaiser model called the Safari was built especially for Clyde Beatty, the famed African hunter and wild-animal trainer, shown here with the car. The interior trim was made of genuine lion and zebra skin.

The cowboy singing star, Gene Autry (left), appears again, this time taking delivery of a 1952 Cadillac Sixty Special.

Pinin Farina (standing), Italy's premier automobile coach-builder and designer, came to Detroit in April 1951 to get the reactions of Nash-Kelvinator president George W. Mason (at the wheel) to a new custom body he had created for the Nash-Healey sports car. Mason was delighted with the clean lines in the Farina tradition, and limited production began soon after, replacing an earlier design which incorporated a Healey body. Nash Ambassador engines and drivelines were shipped from Kenosha, Wisconsin to England where they were modified by the Donald Healey company, then shipped to Turin, Italy where Farina added custom aluminum bodies. The completed cars then were shipped to America. The Nash-Healey was expensive, as a result, but the program helped build the Nash image as an innovator.

Campaigning in South Bend, Indiana for the presidency
in the summer of 1952, Dwight D. Eisenhower rode in a
Studebaker Commander convertible. Loyal South Benders
cheered both the former general and war hero and the
automobile, a South Bend product.

This unusual photograph, taken in Washington with the
Capitol in the background, shows President Dwight D.
Eisenhower waving happily, as a wary Secret Service agent
looks at a crowd we cannot see. He is riding in a 1953
Cadillac convertible, one of the official White House cars.

Veteran film actor Gilbert Roland was making the picture
Thunder Bay when he took time out to be photographed
with a 1953 Cadillac coupe de ville. Born Luis Antonio
Damaso de Alonso in Mexico in 1905, he was a popular
Latin lover of both the silent and sound screen. One of his
first successes was as Armand in the silent version of
Camille, opposite Norma Talmadge, in 1927.

Smiling prettily from a 1953 Packard convertible is Rita
Moreno, Puerto Rican-born Hollywood actress who
appeared in fifteen movies from 1950 to 1963, including
The King and I in 1956 and **West Side Story** in 1961.
She is not to be confused with Rosita Moreno, shown
earlier with a 1930 Franklin.

Waving from the 1954 Dodge convertible that paced the Indianapolis 500 race on May 31, 1954 are Jerry Lewis and Dean Martin. They formed a partnership, one of the most phenomenal successes in the history of show business, soon after meeting in Atlantic City in 1946. They played to packed houses in night clubs and theaters all around the United States, then were hugely successful with live and filmed performances on television and in sixteen motion pictures they made together. They dissolved their partnership in 1966, and each went his own way to carve a separate new career.

Popular singing star Dinah Shore is fascinated by the experimental Chevrolet Corvair exhibited at the GM Motorama in New York in 1954. Thomas H. Keating, Chevrolet general manager, stands behind the car. Miss Shore, born in Winchester, Tennessee in 1917, became a leading singer on radio in the late 1930s. While she made six motion pictures from 1943 to 1952, her greatest success was on television.

When this photograph of John Bromfield with his 1954 Nash Metropolitan was taken in 1954, he was starring with Martha Vickers in United Artists' **The Big Bluff.** Later he starred in the TV series, "The Sheriff of Cochise," and its sequel, "U.S. Marshal." The Metropolitan was built by Austin and Fisher-Ludlow in England and sold by Nash and American Motors dealers in the U.S. and Canada from 1954 to 1962. Close to 100,000 convertibles and hardtops were produced.

*Film actress Jane Russell is admiring the 1954 Cadillac she has just purchased. A native of Bemidji, Minnesota, she made her first picture **The Outlaw** in 1940. It was produced by Howard Hughes. She also starred in **The Paleface** in 1948 and **The Tall Men** in 1955.*

Discussing the new 1954 Kaiser-Darrin sports car with a Kaiser-Frazer salesman at an automobile show is Dave Garroway, the popular radio and television personality. He hosted the "Monitor" show on NBC Radio for years, and in 1962 became the first host on the "Today" program on NBC Television. The Kaiser-Darrin, which had sliding doors and a fiberglass body, was designed by Howard "Dutch" Darrin. A total of 435 was produced.

*In New York, Columbia Pictures' crew prepares to shoot a scene for the film **The Solid Gold Cadillac,** in which Paul Douglas presents Judy Holliday with a solid gold 1955 Cadillac convertible. Douglas (1907-1959) was a radio sportscaster and announcer before he played the scrap tycoon in **Born Yesterday,** which had a long Broadway run. Judy Holliday (1922-1965) played the shrewd blonde in **Born Yesterday** and recreated the role in the 1950 screen version which won for her an Academy Award.*

Smiling at the door of a 1955 Dodge LaFemme hardtop is Mary Costa, best remembered for her appearance in numerous Chrysler Corporation television commercials in the late 1950s. She also was in one motion picture, **The Big Caper,** in 1957.

Red Skelton, the popular giggling comedian who starred on radio and television for many years, takes a picture of the cameraman taking a picture of him and his family as they take delivery of a new 1955 Cadillac Eldorado. Skelton also starred in thirty-two motion pictures from 1941 to 1965.

Pacing the auto industry in its move toward higher performance and greater emphasis on horsepower in 1955 was Chevrolet which boasted a powerful V-8, its first all-new engine since 1929. Pacing the Indianapolis 500-mile race that year was this Chevrolet convertible, driven by Thomas H. Keating, Chevrolet general manager. His passenger is Tony Hulman, Speedway owner. Standing is Mauri Rose, who competed in the 500 fifteen times and was co-winner of the 1941 classic and winner in 1947 and 1948.

DAIMLER-BENZ A.G.

King Gustav II of Sweden, is pictured standing in his 1955 Mercedes-Benz 300. He became king at the age of sixty-eight in 1950, and died in 1973 at ninety-one.

Comedian Bob Hope came to South Bend, Indiana on September 27, 1954 to take part in the introduction to Studebaker Corporation employees of the company's new line of cars and trucks. He is talking to Dale Kellar, a Studebaker employee who is driving a President hardtop model. The President series was revived in 1955 after a lapse of thirteen years.

With newsmen in its wake, the experimental 1956 LeSabre moves down the pavement at the General Motors technical center in Warren, Michigan. At the wheel is Harley Earle, GM styling chief, and his passenger (with his arm on the door sill) is Indonesia's first president, Sukarno. Like many other Indonesians, he had no first name. The LeSabre was one of a bevy of experimental "idea" cars shown across the country by GM in the 1950s.

Actor Jim Davis stands beside a 1956 Studebaker Hawk. It was the first year for the sports-type car which was built through the 1964 model year. In one of his first film roles, Davis co-starred with Bette Davis in **Winter Meeting** in 1948. He appeared in two 1956 pictures, **The Maverick Queen** and **The Bottom of the Bottle.** Davis also had a successful career in television. He played in the popular "Dallas" series.

General Motors president Harlow H. Curtice waves from the driver's seat of the experimental Firebird II. The gas-turbine car was the star of GM's Motorama, held in January 1956 at New York's Waldorf-Astoria Hotel. The Motorama later was on view in Miami, Los Angeles, San Francisco and Boston. The Firebird name later was given to a high-performance Pontiac model.

Lyndon B. Johnson, when he was serving as United States senator from Texas, owned this 1957 Imperial crown limousine, the top luxury model offered by Chrysler Corporation.

Can it be Richard Nixon in an Edsel? It is. The picture was taken in 1958 in Lima, Peru as the Vice-President of the United States waved from a slowly-moving Edsel convertible. Later, he was bombarded with eggs, tomatoes and bricks as unhappy Latins let him know what they thought of relations between Peru and the U.S. The Edsel was an unsuccessful attempt by Ford Motor Company to broaden its share of the medium-priced field. The car with the controversial radiator design and garish trim was marketed in the three-year period from 1958 to 1960 and then dropped. Within a few years, a cult began to develop among some Edsel lovers, who formed the Edsel Owners Club which at this writing has more than 2,000 members. The club's enthusiastic founder, Perry E. Piper, of West Liberty, Illinois, provided this photograph of "one loser with another." Piper recalls that as the result of having met Nixon during the 1972 campaign, following the president's visit to the Illinois State Fair, Nixon agreed to autograph the original picture.

236

*Actress Debbie Reynolds pauses from her filming of **This Happy Feeling** to pose happily with her 1958 Dual-Ghia, a limited-edition, high-performance bucket-seated tourer favored by the elite of Hollywood. From 1955 to 1958 a total of 104 were turned out by Dual Motors Corporation of Detroit. Body work was by Ghia in Italy, with the engine and most other components supplied by Chrysler Corporation.*

*Fresh from her success in the motion picture **Soyonara** is the talented star Miiko Taka, seated on the hood of a 1958 Cadillac convertible. Other films in which she subsequently appeared include **Hell to Eternity** in 1960, **Cry for Happy** in 1961 and **The Art of Love** in 1965.*

Lawrence Welk and members of his orchestra pose with a 1959 Dodge Custom Royal convertible at a California dealership. Welk had one of the most popular dance bands in the 1930s and 1940s, and he achieved remarkable success with a weekly television program on the air until the 1980s. In 1959 he was sponsored on TV by Dodge.

George Romney, president of American Motors Corporation, is pictured with two Rambler models that helped the company establish alltime production and sales records in 1959. Largely due to Romney's evangelical zeal in championing the cause of the compact car in which his company pioneered, AMC produced 374,240 automobiles in the 1959 model year, the highest mark for any U.S. independent auto manufacturer in history. The record was broken several times in succeeding years by AMC.

*One of America's alltime dancing and singing stars, Fred Astaire, turns on his famous smile as he poses with a 1960 Imperial. Born in Omaha, Nebraska in 1899 as Frederick Austerlitz, he toured the vaudeville circuit at seven with his sister as a dancing partner. Their first big success on Broadway was in **The Passing Show of 1918.** They went on to become perennial favorites with Broadway and London audiences. Astaire moved to Hollywood in the early 1930s and won fame in ten musicals with Ginger Rogers. In addition to being a skillful dancer, he won applause for the many hit songs he introduced that were written especially for his voice.*

Former President Harry Truman takes delivery of a new 1960 Dodge Polara in Kansas City, Missouri. Handing him the keys is Dodge general manager Matthew C. Patterson. The author for many years served with Patterson on the board of directors of Goodwill Industries of Greater Detroit.

Standing in the official 1961 Lincoln Continental presidential limousine is President John F. Kennedy. The front section of the bubbletop has been removed. The Lincoln, custom-built by Hess and Eisenhardt of Cincinnati, Ohio, is the same car in which President Kennedy was riding when he was assassinated on November 22, 1963. On that occasion the bubbletop also had been removed. After the tragic events in Dallas, the car was rebuilt in 1964 and was used by Presidents Johnson, Nixon, Ford and Carter. It then was retired and was presented to the Henry Ford Museum in Dearborn, Michigan.

Ian Fleming, the talented British creator of the famous James Bond novels, gets into his 1963 Studebaker Avanti. He was the original author of seven highly successful motion pictures of the 1960s, including **Dr. No** and **Goldfinger.**

INDIANAPOLIS MOTOR SPEEDWAY

CHRYSLER HISTORICAL COLLECTION

Pacing the 1964 Indianapolis 500 race is a Ford Mustang convertible driven by Benson Ford, vice-president of the Ford Motor Company. His passenger is Tony Hulman, president of the Indianapolis Motor Speedway. One of the most successful cars ever introduced, the Mustang was the first of many "pony cars" brought out in the 1960s by the U.S. manufacturers. Most touted high performance and youthful styling.

Her handsome 1966 Imperial has just returned from a shopping trip to bring Ginger Rogers back to the Broadway theater where she is starring in **Hello, Dolly!** The versatile star of Hollywood films for three decades began her career on Broadway, in **Girl Crazy,** in the early 1930s. She made ten unforgettable pictures with Fred Astaire, including **Roberta** and **Top Hat** in 1935 and **Shall We Dance** in 1937. She won an Oscar for her performance in **Kitty Foyle** in 1940.

FORD MOTOR COMPANY

Carroll Shelby stands with two of the 1968 Cobra sports cars that bear his name. Shelby was president of Shelby Automotive which built the Ford-powered Shelby Cobra and Shelby Mustang in California. Both were sold by franchised Ford dealers. In 1982 Shelby began producing the Shelby Charger for Chrysler Corporation.

The keys to an all-pink 1968 AMX sports car are presented by R. W. McNealey, an American Motors vice-president, to Angela Dorian of Los Angeles, chosen "Playmate of the Year" by the readers of **Playboy** magazine. The two-seater AMX, built in the model years 1968 to 1970, proved so popular it later spawned an enthusiasts organization called the Classic AMX Club International, whose members own restored AMX cars that are shown at collector car meets around the country.

GM PHOTOGRAPHIC

O. J. Simpson, the fabulous rushing back of college and professional football, poses with a 1969 Camaro, Chevrolet's highly successful "pony car," introduced in 1967 and at this writing, still running as effectively as O. J.

Mark Donohue is pictured with a red-white-and-blue Javelin AMX similar to the one he drove to the Sports Car Club of America's Trans-American Championship in 1971. Donohue also drove a Sunoco Javelin to victory three times in the 1970 Trans-Am series. Winner of the Indianapolis 500 in 1972, Donohue died in August 1975 in Graz, Austria of injuries received in a Grand Prix race.

Richard Nixon, with his wife Pat, was a happy man on the day of his second inauguration in January 1973. They are shown here in the Lincoln limousine in which President John F. Kennedy was assassinated in 1963. The car, originally a 1961 model, was completely rebuilt at a cost of far above a million dollars and was used by Presidents Johnson, Nixon, Ford and Carter before its retirement.

Farrah Fawcett was starring in the television program "Charlie's Angels" when this photograph of her taking delivery of a 1977 Cougar XR-7 was taken. She also starred in Mercury Cougar TV commercials for several years. John B. Vanderzee, Lincoln-Mercury advertising manager, is giving her a silver pendant, similar to the one she wore in the commercials with a likeness of the snarling cougar hood ornament.

It is fitting that the last photograph to appear in **Cars With Personalities** be of a 1982 automobile. It is even more appropriate that the car is a faithful reproduction of one of the great classics of the past — a Duesenberg II speedster, the latest creation of Elite Heritage Motors Corporation of Elroy, Wisconsin. At the wheel is the Republican governor of Wisconsin, Lee Sherman Dreyfus.

The Duesenberg II is a replica of the 1933 Duesenberg SJ speedster, designed originally by Gordon Buehrig. Its price is $101,000. Elite Heritage, according to its president, Richard I. Braund, delivered its first Duesenberg reproduction in October 1978. Since that time, through August 1982, the company has sold twenty-seven hand-crafted cars, each of which required more than 5,000 man hours to build.

Index

Design and typesetting (in Goudy Old
Style) by American Center Studios,
Southfield, Michigan. Printed and
bound by R. R. Donnelley & Sons
Company at Crawfordsville, Indiana.